LOCH NESS

By the same Author
Maxwell's Ghost
Beyond The Highland Line

LOCH NESS

Richard Frere

John Murray

© Richard Frere 1988

First published in 1988
by John Murray (Publishers) Ltd
50 Albemarle Street, London WIX 4BD

Typeset by Chapterhouse
Printed and bound in Great Britain
by Butler & Tanner, Frome and London

British Library Cataloguing in Publication Data

Frere, Richard, *1922–*
  Loch Ness
  1. Scotland.   Highland Region.   Loch Ness
  region to 1988
  I. Title
  941.1'75

ISBN 0–7195–4598–6

Contents

Illustration Acknowledgements

The Author 14, 16, 18, 22–23, 27, 28, 29, 31, 33, 48–49, 66–67, 100, 102–103, 113, 115, 119, 120–121, 123, 124–125, 130, 155, 161; BBC Hulton Picture Library 24, 39, 61, 82; Dr Nicholas Dixon (artist: Lyn Mason) 36; *Scottish Field* 43; Her Majesty The Queen 53, 75; private Scottish collection 56; Scottish National Portrait Gallery 59; National Library of Scotland 71 (Culloden); *The Highland News* 73; Mr Donald M Mackay 74, 76–77; Curtis Brown Ltd 81; British Waterways Board 91; Real Photography Co 95; The Forestry Commission 99; *Aberdeen Press and Journal* 106; The Late Mr. J. A. Menzies, Drumnadrochit 134–135, 137; R. T. Holmes 140; British Aerospace 142–143; Loch Ness Wellington Association Ltd 145; Ivor Newby 148, 149, 150, 152, 170; North of Scotland Hydro-Electric Board 156, 158, 159; British Museum (Natural History) 173

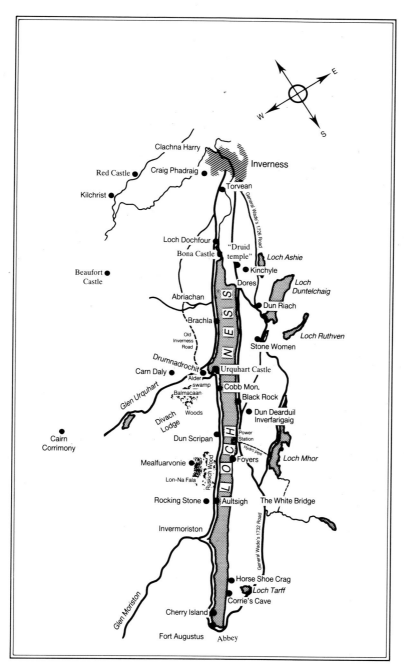

Loch Ness and its surrounds

1   *The Great Fracture*

ROCKS ARE the underlying bones of any countryside and to understand them helps one to appreciate the flesh more fully. I am no geologist, but, as a climber, have a touching acquaintance with my subject, so I shall have to keep my description simple, or make a fool of myself. Loch Ness, then, is a substantial body of water some twenty-four miles long by around a mile wide; at its deepest it goes down nearly a thousand feet, and is estimated to hold 263,000 million cubic feet of water. It occupies a large part of the Great Glen fault which indisputably extends from the coastline of the Black Isle in the east to Loch Linnhe in the west. My teachers hint that this fault was in existence in pre-Cambrian times which means it is about 700 million years old, and at no time in its long life has it been truly at rest. Uneasy earth movements, for instance, were the cause of no less than fifty-six earthquakes along and around it from 1768 to 1906. There was a considerable tremour in 1934 which I remember well, as a boy in Inverness. The big Victorian wardrobe in my bedroom creaked and groaned, and it felt as though someone were tapping the legs of my bed with a mallet. My father who had spent his best years in the Far East knew all about such events, and told me the why and wherefore of it. Half fascinated, half nervous, I spent much of the following day reading about the San Francisco earthquake, since that city paid the penalty of being built upon an active fault. The great earthquake that destroyed and flooded Lisbon in 1755 sent out shock waves that were felt as far north as Norway and agitated the waters of Loch Ness. Some reports suggest that a 'seiche' condition was set up in which the water rolled from one end of the loch to the other.

The length and singular straightness of the Great Glen had long attracted unpublished comment before Sir R. Murchison and Sir A. Geekie sagely observed to the Geological Society in 1861 that 'the fracture was more extensive than any other in the country'. This somewhat ponderous pronouncement was followed in 1914 by the bland remark of Messrs. Horne and Hinxman that the fault was essentially normal; the land to the east had simply slipped down a few thousand feet with the passage of time.

This was a plain enough theory but its very simplicity made it suspect. There were prominent clues to a much greater complexity in the form of widely separated yet matching rock types on either side of the cleft. In 1946 W. Q. Kennedy came out with a brand new theory. Briefly, his proposition was that the fissure had cracked open and moved *sideways*. Apart from its attenuated length he used the fact that the surrounding rocks were shattered and broken over a wide area (between 1½ and 2½ miles) on each side. This he knew to be characteristic of faults in other parts of the world that had moved, or were still moving sideways. Such faults are called 'transcurrent' which is a confusing word for sideways.

Kennedy came to the conclusion that this event had taken place 400 million years ago. He was struck by the fact that there are two massive intrusions of granite on either side of the Great Glen sixty-five miles apart. (Granite is molten rock that has risen up through the crust of the earth and then cooled and hardened below the surface. Thereafter it has been exposed by erosion.) Specifically Kennedy matched the granite at Foyers half-way down the east side of Loch Ness with that at Strontian on Loch Linnhe. If he were right it would mean that, in those distant days, the village of Dores at the north-eastern end of the Loch (had it then existed) would have been physically twinned with Oban (had it also been there). That's a mind-boggling concept, no doubt; but looking from a remote past to an equally distant future they tell us that if the movement along the St Andreas Fault in California continues at its present jerky snail's pace San Francisco and Los Angeles will be side-by-side in 50 million years or so.

So, in cosmic terms, Kennedy's conclusion must have sounded quite feasible, but interest in the great fault was growing and it was soon disputed. S. J. Shand, five years later, was concerned by the fact that after a thorough search he was unable to find any evidence of sideways scouring and not much sign of mylonite. My dictionary defines mylonite as 'a fine grained metamorphic (altered) rock . . . formed by the crushing, grinding and rolling of the original structure'. Its presence would certainly seem to be a pointer to a theory of abrasion on the grand scale.

But Shand's objection came under objection in its turn. V. A. Eyles and A. G. MacGregor in a paper in the *Geological Magazine* in 1952 outlined a detailed field study of the lochside rocks which showed the existence of a forty-mile long belt of intense pulverisation and much more of the significant mylonite than Shand had found. For some nine years the disputatious voices fell silent and when they resumed it was more to discuss the overall length of the fault than the history of its movements. To the north east it was finally projected as far as Spitsbergen, and

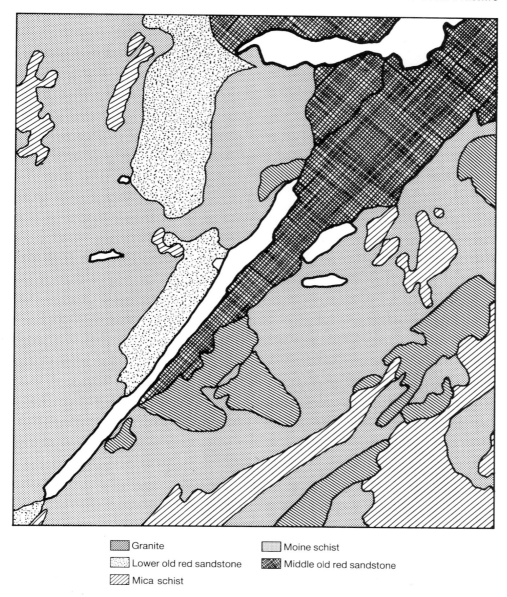

	Granite		Moine schist
	Lower old red sandstone		Middle old red sandstone
	Mica schist		

The geology of Loch Ness

south west, to Newfoundland. The self-explanatory word 'megashear' was used to describe this monster crack.

The introduction of isotopic dating cast a bright light on the dark subject of the age of rocks. This science makes use of the radio activity within a rock's structure; given the amount of the radio active element present, and the amount of radio active decay, then (the rate of decay being constant and known) the age can be arrived at. Armed with this technique M. U. Ahmad found reasons to doubt Kennedy's theory that the Foyers and Strontian granite outcrops once formed a single mass. He had discovered radioactive differences between the minerals in the two groups. But R. J. Marston replied that such objections could be explained by varied levels of erosion, and he came out strongly on Kennedy's side.

And so it went on. By 1969 N. Holgate had gone deeply into the matter. With his area of investigation extending from Mull to the Moray Firth coast and by examining every relevant factor, he sought to show that there had been two major fault movements separated by some 250 million years. He agreed with Kennedy that the first movement had been sinistral (i.e. motion to the left, as observed from the far side of the fault) but thought it greater in extent: some eighty-three miles. Then much later, in Eocene times, just when the great reptiles so mysteriously vanished, the weary rocks ground slowly back, moving in all eighteen miles to the right until they took up approximately their present position. Give or take a few miles (and some moments of geological time) it wasn't so different from what Kennedy had said.

Garson and Plant in 1972 took an opposite view, literally. They made an apparently convincing case for two movements in a dextral (motion to the right) direction. And others have had other ideas. Indeed, from the 1970s, a certain light-hearted element seems to have entered into the discussion. Using a variety of detective tricks – the chronology of earth events, the study of altered rocks, properties of magnetism, etc. – artful geologists have tried to mate scanty facts with a plethora of theory. I myself have to admit to a growing obsession, in my small, uninformed way, with the Geological Survey Ten Mile Map (North Sheet) that is pinned on my study wall. I can sit for hours trying to fit the badly broken pieces of the jigsaw together. As a child, blindfold and excited, one used to try to place the tail on the donkey. Is there an analogy here?

Nowadays, at least, the Loch lies quietly enough between the steep wooded sides of the fault. The rocks which are exposed in its crags, gullies, excavations and beaches (and which form the building blocks of its older houses) are representative in some form or another of all three groups that make up the Earth's crust. The igneous, the metamorphic and the sedimentary lie in an almost orderly fashion around the Loch; compared with, for instance, Loch Maree, the geological pattern seems simple and is perhaps responsible for the plain topography which we see today.

A drive or, if you have the time and energy, a walk round the Loch will take you through all these zones. The village of Dores, on the B 852 road, is a good place to start. Dores stands on a bed of Old Red Sandstone which covers a large area south of Inverness and the Black Isle and continues discontinuously up the east coast as far as Caithness. This sedimentary rock, the hard, compacted, current state of eroded material, weathered, washed and blown from the high ground to the west over millions of years is now of immense depth. Though it attains a height of over 2000 feet above the Loch it was once at the bottom of the sea. At Lochan an Eoin Ruadha, two miles south of Dores, fossil fragments of fish and plants have been found. The buckling of the underlying 'pavement' rock in a succession of geological periods is responsible for this massive rearrangement.

The sandstone extends in a narrow belt as far as Foyers. Near Inverfarigaig a spectacular gully cuts into the hill, and at the Black Rock a steep cliff, blasted over two hundred years ago by General Wade's engineers to make a way for his road, drops right down to the water. This gives a close-up view of the sandstone, which has here formed what is known as a conglomerate rock. This structure has been created by stones and debris eroded from long-vanished cliffs becoming embedded in the soft grains and eventually hardening into a solid mass.

Such outcrops of conglomerate rock are conspicuous features of the high country above Dores, known locally as the Inverness Lake District. Rising from the gravel-fringed lochs of Ashie, Ceo Glais and Loch a' Choire (tucked away within a ring of reddish, terraced cliffs) the flat-topped, shaggy hills with their sudden bluffs look, side on, like sleeping bears with black noses. But if you go near to them these exposed portions of the Earth immediately invite another comparison, and you may think them the work of a builder who has mixed a great quantity of concrete and then dumped it on the moor to harden.

As a boy, with other boys, I used to bicycle to these small cliffs on hot summer evenings and climb on them, constantly and obsessively. After fifty years I can still remember that first and special touch, the exploratory, sensual handling of smooth, rounded stone, the testing of tiny excrescences and the satisfaction of the huge, incut socket from which a large pebble had been prised by rain or frost. Lying on the moors or on the lower slopes of the hills, these bluffs are invariably mossy and lichenous and the scraping away of these growths produced a scent like that of old tweed, pungent and highly evocative. I can recall, also, dangerous moments, hanging on small holds with no visible holds above, the sweating fingers, the trembling toes, the way down quite forgotten in the panic, but these were the heady days of initiation which became the stuff of rose-coloured, abiding memory.

The traveller on the A 82 road, fresh from the conglomerate Black Rock, is presented at Wade's bridge over the River Farigaig with the almost overpowering

Loch Ness

Dun Dearduil, a sweeping grey precipice much older than the rocks which surround it. The Dun is partly composed of Moine schist, an altered (metamorphic) rock that can be split into thin layers. It is a worn-down remnant, a relic of the time when these schists covered the area to a depth of three or four miles! South-east of Foyers is an intruded mass of granite which supports, among other substantial features, Loch Mhor, the reservoir for the pumped-storage plant there. This granite bubbled up in molten (igneous) form some 400 million years ago and cooled below that same monstrous roof, but erosion has humbled the casing and the encased alike. This is known to the initiated as a 'batholith' and, if Mr Kennedy and his supporters are right, once formed a single mass with the granite at Strontian.

From Foyers to Fort Augustus the student of Loch Ness-side geology must proceed on foot over some very rough terrain; the road veers away from the Loch and loops over the hills to the south. The ten miles along the shore is an adventure, a pebbly promenade beneath steep slopes of bramble, birch and hazel, and huge spills of scree. For the most part the rock here is Moine schist but opposite Invermoriston there is another intrusion of granite, less massive than its neighbour but I *Horseshoe Crag* suppose of joint origin.

This lonely bank is seamed by burns and small rivers which tumble steeply to Loch Ness, draining such lochs as Kemp, Knockie, and Tarff through ravines harshly excavated by the glacial floodwaters that followed successive Ice Ages. To me it is a source of lasting amazement that the latest of these episodes ended a mere 10,000 years ago and that a new one may be even now beginning. It quite upsets a cosy feeling that, if we discount man's perverse activities, we have a safe, solid and lasting world with an environment pretty well suited to our needs. I have the same feeling of instability when I remember that our planet's skin of wholesome air is less than five miles thick. These are reminders of how narrowly we are tolerated and give one no reason whatsoever for a vote of confidence in the Cosmos.

Beinn a Bhacaidh, some four miles from Fort Augustus as a crow might fly, is the highest hill on the south side of the Loch and is a prominent landmark from any point on the shore. It is a ruinous, hump-backed hill with a grey Moine N.W. face which carries the ravages of geological time. The metamorphic rock, warped by successive crustal pressures into easily shattered strata, has been eroded by friction, ice and weather and now lies in extensive scree fields beneath low, truncated outcrops. Gravity has graded the spoil perfectly: from tiny pebbles, at the top to lumps as big as small houses at loch level. Chance arrangement of the distribution has formed the so-called Horseshoe Crag, a sprawling grey shape in the form of an inverted U, which is somehow reminiscent of the Long Man of Wilmington in Sussex.

The hills on the opposite of the Loch are of similar formation though generally smoother. The contorted strata is conspicuous at road cuttings between Fort Augustus and Invermoriston, and above the latter place a dramatic precipice, the Sron na Muic, hangs above the village. It is matched by Craig nan Eun on the opposite side of the glen mouth. There is much evidence here of erosion by ice at the time when the ice cap was pushing its slow but irresistible weight to the east. On a hill called Creag Lundie, a few miles up Glen Moriston, are some wonderful examples of ice-sculptured rock. The exposed faces rise, tier upon tier, to the top of the hill. With hardly a visible seam or joint the ground and polished surfaces look, from a little distance, more like sheets of steel than the bared bones of Earth. In an odd way it is disturbing, as is anything that closely resembles an artefact but is obviously nothing of the kind.

The action of ice has had an enormous influence upon the present topography of the Great Glen. Because glaciers and ice caps still exist elsewhere in the world it is possible to form an idea of the nature of the vast sheet that enshrouded the Scottish Highlands to a depth of almost four thousand feet a million years ago. Before that, for successive ages, the climate had been equable, not unlike what it is today. Then the air began to cool. In our Highlands the hills were rounder and with less character, like fat, inexperienced faces; the valleys were narrower than they are now. The winter snows began to linger, even on the lower mountains, until well into summer. As the weather grew even colder the snowfalls accumulated at all levels until there was no thaw anywhere at all. Under such circumstances the gradual establishment of a great ice cap was inevitable. Eventually it spread under its own weight and spawned glaciers that edged their ways downwards through faults and river valleys. The Great Glen was a major depository for the ice which flowed east into the basin of the Moray Firth. Slowly, stealthily yet inexorably the glacier ploughed its way down the great fault, excavating, bulldozing, and pushing huge quantities of sand, gravel and boulders before its snout. Like the Mills of God it ground exceeding small and the sand and shingle it deposited in the Ness valley is

The Author's artificial pond

over three hundred feet deep. Superficially it also left its mark in the form of the eskers (winding ridges formed under melting ice) of Tomnahurich and Torvean which dominate the town of Inverness.

When finally, around 18,000 years ago, the latest of the great freezes began to relent, the flow of ice in the Glen (and elsewhere) halted, vacillated and then began to melt in earnest. In due course the higher summits came out of glassy darkness to bask once again in the kindly sun. The ice shrank from the rocks that it had so thoroughly pulverised, the virgin glitter of its surface now stained with dust and sand. A warmer wind and drenching rain sent rivulets of water down the ice which combined to form rushing streams. It was the beginning of the post-glacial flood.

In my garden here I have dug, over the years, an artificial pond. It is both a pleasure and an education, the latter since it demonstrates, in microcosm, the principles of erosion by water. My pond, some twenty yards square, is supplied by an aquaduct from an adjacent stream that is blocked by a small dam. A thirty-foot long ditch, narrow when originally dug, connects the end of the aquaduct with the pond. The stream, which I have tapped for my aquatics, has its source in a loch, three miles distant, which drains a wide area of elevated moorland; so it readily responds to rainfall. In all seasons my pond is interesting, but mostly so during an early Spring thaw. In Drumnadrochit January and February are usually dry and frosty but considerable snow may build up on the hills. In the sandstone bed of my stream the water has died by then to a trickle and small icicles decorate the walls. Ice too has driven its wedges between the sandstone layers and split them. The broken pieces hang as if supported by a temporary glue.

Sometime in March the night frosts end, the barometer falls, the blue sky becomes tarnished with yellow-grey, the cold-sweating ground is squalid. A south-west wind (colder, to the body, than any frost) brings a drenching rain and on the hilly moors the toy icecap begins to melt. At intervals, during the progress of the thaw, I go down to the pond to watch.

Within a very few hours the trickle turns to a torrent. Where the stream bends, the flood water, already dense with spoil, volleys against the banks and brings down frost-weakened rocks. The pond fills rapidly with thick brown water. In my linking ditch (two feet wide in 1970, now nearly ten) medium boulders jostle each other with a subfluvial rumbling and release more silt into the water. However prolonged the rain the water is usually running clear within forty-eight hours. By then the bed of my pond is covered by a thin deposit of dull yellow sand and peat. In toto it doesn't amount to much, nor is the rocky bed of the stream much changed; but it was done in less than two days, and by a single small stream.

Ten thousand years ago the glaciers had almost vanished from the hanging corries that they had carved. They had also been responsible for narrowed ridges, roughly gouged out ravines, flat-bottomed valleys, and millions of tons of commercial sand and gravels: in fact, an entirely new topography. They left their little curiosities too, in the shape of 'erratics', single boulders or beds of rock of different composition from that in their new locality. They had been carried from afar and dumped by the melting ice.

Regional land masses, freed from the weight of the icecap, gradually began to recover. The sea, brimming with meltwater, rose too, more rapidly, by over two hundred feet. In our area Loch Ness arguably formed part of a salt-water channel that extended from coast to coast until the emerging land and the massive silt deposits in the Ness Valley brought about its present land-locked condition.

Loch Ness

One supposes that the snow line, that point above which there is no thaw, only gradually rose to its present altitudinal level over Scotland. Perhaps there was a transitional time when the 1500 ft. summits around Loch Ness glittered brilliantly in an August noonday sun. It is not so today. Yet within a mere thirty miles of the loch, high on the face of Ben Nevis, is a tiny patch that never melts. So small by the summer's end that a man may sit on it and not leave room for a companion, it is a minute, obstinate reminder of the time, not so *very* long ago, when this mountain, the Great Glen, and most of Scotland were embedded invisibly in a block of ice nearly half as deep as that which covers Greenland.

Moved by the iceman's rare work on Craig Lundie I have digressed from my description of the existing rock forms immediately around Loch Ness. The Moine rocks continue to flank the loch for about two miles east of Invermoriston before giving way to a belt of Old Red Sandstone (Lower, as opposed to Middle on the

The Author and the rocking stone (see p. 20)

other side of the Loch) which extends right round into and slightly beyond Glenur-quhart. The passage through this zone by the A 82 main road has been, in the years gone by, potentially hazardous because of the great amount of loose rock left by the blasting when the A 82 road was realigned and widened in the 1930s. The sand-stone here is different from that between Dores and Foyers; if that can be compared to concrete, then this is pure cement. It is a softish rock and its beds slope mostly downwards towards the road. Although the climate so close to the water is rela-tively mild it is not frost-free and, being south-facing, is quickly warmed by the sun. This is a condition well known and justly feared by climbers on, for example, the North Face of the Eiger. The rocks, already shaken and cracked by the road makers, are all too ready to slide down their neighbours' backs. Frost which expands the joints and water which washes down superficial shale and mud, are the joint agents of destruction.

A man used to bicycle daily beneath these artificial cliffs, removing stones that had fallen onto the road. His was a secure employment, with no obvious end to it in sight. Nowadays he has become motorised and his job has recently been simplified by the Roads Department's provision of steel nets to contain the most unstable parts of the face. It is a timely move; the decay of the sandstone cliffs is progressive. Apart from bombardment by single boulders – some large enough to leave dents in the tarmacadam – this section of the A 82 has several times been blocked by massive landslips. Only a few years ago, when driving home from Spean Bridge late one December night, I was suddenly faced by a mountain of debris right across the road. It was eerie and disorientating to see the familiar form of the surface ending abruptly in a new cliff. The avalanche debris was sufficient to conceal a car, had there been one there; it took several days to clear it, and the spoil provided ample material for the foundations of a new lay-by which now can be seen opposite a deep, concave scoop in the hillside.

High above these cuttings and invisible from the road squats Mealfuarvonie, the Loch's loftiest hill. Its bulk, memorable shape and isolated situation make it appear higher than its 2284 feet. It is a conglomerate giant with sandstone feet. Its claim to geological fame is the fact that here the formation reaches a higher level than almost anywhere else in the country. In altitude Morven, in Caithness, has a few more feet but it lacks its rival's bulk. From the N.E. and S.W. Mealfuarvonie is con-spicuous from miles away as a symmetrical dome but it is actually a long ridge, run-ning parallel to Loch Ness, with sheer sides. It has the marked characteristics of the smaller conglomerate hills across the Loch; a flat top, abrupt terraced cliffs, and deep, dank serpentine cracks and fissures. Representing the south-west limit of the Old Red Sandstone it is faulted from the extensive Moine rocks of the Balmacaan Forest. This area contains several hills that are not much lower than the Meal but their metamorphic bodies give them a completely different appearance.

Between the Loch and Mealfuarvonie there is a gently sloping moor called the Lon na Fola. It occupies most of the platform of small-grained sandstone which supports the great conglomerate ridge/dome. The streams that run across the Lon are slow moving and their beds are shallow; the water glides rather than gurgles between tile-thin wafers of ochre rock. Where there are no faults for them to bite into, the streams seem to have made little impression on the rock, but at joints and weaknesses it is a different story. Where Moine meets sandstone at Allt Sigh, three miles N.E. of Invermoriston, there is a massive ravine while at Divach, south of Drumnadrochit, a large burn cascades into a deep gorge at the broken fringe of the same conjunction.

Mention of Allt Sigh reminds me that on Meall na Sroine, on the Moine side of the ravine, is an entertaining reminder of Ice Age removals – a large round rock weighing several tons and at the same time so perfectly balanced that a touch of the finger can set it rocking. It is an 'erratic' which must have been rolled and tumbled from the east before, somehow or other, finding its final resting place on the very edge of the Great Glen.

The villages of Drumnadrochit and Lewiston occupy the north-east corner of the oblong block of Lower Old Red sandstone that includes Mealfuarvonie. The burns and rivers at the mouth of Glenurquhart run smoothly over dark, rosy slabs scoured and polished by ice-borne gravel and eroded conglomerates. All around is evidence of the glacial tongues that forced their way into Loch Ness through the bounding hills. The conspicuous tree-clad outcrops of Creag Monie and Creag Ney are tough conglomerate structures that have partly resisted the force of the ice. The post-glacial raising of the land has left 'beaches' (very obvious on the south side of the glen above Lewiston) from the times when the great melts inundated the area. It is fascinating to compare, in miniature and short term, the effects of artificially altered levels on the shore line of hydro-electric reservoirs. The Glen's two rivers, the Coiltie and the Enrick, which converge in an alluvial swamp have loaded the rocky bed of Urquhart Bay with a great thickness of eroded material. Even more striking are the warped subaqueous contours at Foyers which show a fan of silt extending half way across the Loch below the delta on which the old British Aluminium Works were built.

Just east of Drumnadrochit the Old Red Sandstone gives way to Moine rock which flanks the Loch as far as Abriachan where a massive intrusion of granite forms the ruinous precipice of Creag Dhearg. Between these two places, above the Clansman Hotel at Brackla, an energetic stream has found the line of a granite-filled fault and descends to the Loch through a narrow, hanging fissure headed by a graceful waterfall. Massive shattering has occurred here in the flanking Moine rocks which, jarred by the movements of the Great Glen Fault and baked by the great heat of the intrusion, are constantly crashing down.

At Creag Dhearg decay, past and present, is on a much bigger scale, and has a different cause. The destructive agency here is chemical; the rock is simply decomposing as the feldspar (an important mineral in granite) is broken down under the rigours of the weather. The crag, an impressive object from the A 82 as one travels east, has recently suffered an immense landslip. A pink scar, like grazed human skin, adorns the south-west face under its hair line of stunted pine; the wound can be seen for miles. The gully into which this avalanche has fallen is formed along a fault that cuts deeply into the back of Carn a Bhodaich (at 1642 ft. the highest point between Drumnadrochit and Inverness) and is a place that I used to visit regularly before the last War with young, like-minded friends. The unreliability of its structure made it highly dangerous but in those days any climbable surface, including trees, gravel pits, walls and the roofs of houses, were obsessively explored.

Having noticed this fresh scar a few years ago, I went to photograph it. At road level the gully is no more than a narrow watercourse but at around 600 ft. it expands into a substantial amphitheatre. The climb to this area is onerous, through birch and hazel thickets, brambly undergrowth and fields of sliding screes. After years of absence I saw considerable changes. Half-way up, a rock fall had blocked the gully and diverted the stream into a new channel. Birch trees had been bruised and splintered by flying boulders, and one venerable specimen had crept downhill, still in a standing position, along with the gravel that gripped its roots. At close quarters the pink scour confirms the distant impression of a major event. Many thousands of tons had been scaled from the face and it gave me a queer feeling to see that a ridge up which we had once habitually climbed no longer existed. Chemical and mechanical weathering of the granite meant no large lumps had survived their collapse into the bed of the gully: the decomposed rock had broken down into small, dusty fragments. I could see that the next spate would carry these away into the bed of Loch Ness.

And so it goes on. Beds of silt, one upon the other, will build under the water until the water itself is displaced. Compressed and dehydrated by its own weight and mixed with cementing minerals, the soft sediment will form new sedimentary rock. Crustal movements – there is life in the old Fault yet – and the accompanying heat may then metamorphose this into an altered crystalline form. When the temperature is sufficiently high the metamorphic phase will be over as the rocks melt and return to an igneous state and thus the cycle is completed.

We have now almost completed our circle of the Loch. The granite buttresses, streaked with browns and greens from their soluble minerals, change to tough Moine rocks again above Lochend and this formation continues in slabby outcrops along the north side of the Great Glen until it is finally buried under the widespread sediments of the Moray Firth basin.

Over: sky and water joining, the Loch extending to Infinity.

A section across the Loch shows that the bottom at around 500 ft. is quite flat and occupies, on average, about its total width. It is a bulbous U shape with outward sloping sides which seem to reflect the angles above water level. A visit to nearby Strathglass, itself formed on a major fault in the Moine schist, will reveal a replica in miniature of that topography; one supposes that, had the River Glass not carved its way through the conglomerate sandstones at Aigas, the Strath would by now accomodate a substantial lake.

There is, in conclusion, another phenomenon which, I think, is singular to Loch Ness. Due to the length and peculiar straightness of the Great Glen fault, it is possible, when standing on the shore at Fort Augustus on a clear day, to see sky and water join. Earth's curvature has drawn the low ground in the Ness Valley below the visible horizon. Though it is commonplace to watch a ship climbing out of the sea, the same effect here is quite startling; at first glance it looks as though the Loch extends to Infinity.

2 The Silent Vanished Races

THE SUCCESSIVE waves of ice that built up over north Britain postponed the human invasion of this area. There is no other reason for the fact that homo sapiens, who had long occupied the narrow, ice-free belt in the southernmost part of the country, didn't arrive in our parts until a mere six thousand years ago. Sound evidence shows that the Oban area, as well as many of the Inner and Outer Hebrides, were colonised by men and women in mesolithic times a millennium earlier, but there is no hint that they came this far east.

These Mesoliths were nomads who lived by hunting and fishing. Their prey was the reindeer (soon to become extinct here) the wild boar, oxen and deer, and the weapons they used were fashioned from bone and stone. They seem to have been tough, resourceful people, skilful in the production of such artefacts, whose short lives (twenty-five years is said to have been the average expectancy) were passed exclusively in the search for food. It is, in fact, by their middens that we know them, and by the great piles of chippings left by their stonemasons. Nothing else remains, which is sad; so much effort and so little left to posterity.

Neolithic man, who occupied the last period of the Stone Age, was different; he didn't have to rely exclusively on hunting and fishing, for the art of growing food was known to him. The practice of agriculture rapidly became widespread. Unlike their rootless predecessors these new immigrants only moved in their search for suitable farming land. When it was found they settled there, at least for a time. And so it was that around six thousand years ago small groups of explorers began to move eastwards from their dwellings around Loch Linnhe. The route through the

Great Glen must have exceeded their most sanguine expectations with its three closely connected lochs for their dug-out canoes and hide-covered coracles. They would have carried their seeds with them and driven their cattle, sheep and goats, although the mind boggles at the task of coaxing livestock along the precipitous, scree-strewn and bramble-infested shorelines of Loch Lochy and Loch Ness. Perhaps the drovers took their herds over the high ground to the south of the Glen.

At any rate it must have been with considerable relief that they reached the blunt gravel beach at Lochend and saw the flat river valley widening to relatively gently sloping moors to the north east. Some families must have settled close to the Loch, in the adjoining Strathnairn, or on the hills between. Others, more adventurous, moved on to where Inverness now stands and turned north to the coasts of Sutherland and Caithness; thence, in due course, even to the far-flung islands of Orkney and Shetland. Our concern is with our local group, and with what little we know about them during their sojourn here. It is sure that they farmed the land after laboriously clearing away the trees, while they still heavily relied on hunting and fishing. Unlike the nomadic, food-catching Mesoliths, who only left their rubbish behind them, this new and semi-landed breed of men found time to raise lasting and prominent monuments to their occupancy. Their massive work can be seen throughout the north, but particularly in Orkney and Shetland. In our area of Loch Ness they are more thin on the ground and only then appear north of a line drawn through the mouth of Glenurquhart. At the head of the Loch, and within the valley of the River Ness, agricultural greed and rural vandalism over the last few hundred years have caused the destruction of many of the monuments so that only dimly discerned outlines remain.

Since man developed an interest in such things these Megalithic tombs have aroused fierce controversy. It is not a bad thing that a few mysteries should remain. The sight of a ring of stones in an empty field, looking like worn-down teeth in a circular jaw, rekindles that sense of wonder and curiosity that ought not to belong exclusively to childhood. I have always wished that I had a neolithic stone circle on my land. If it were in my garden I would prop my spade against it and think of the accumulated effort of six thousand years.

One of the best megalithic tombs in the immediate vicinity of Loch Ness is in upper Glenurquhart. This passage grave in the clachan of Corrimony, consists of a circle of stones some 80 feet in diameter which surround a 50-foot cairn. A central chamber is entered by a short passage at the S.W. Originally this chamber was vaulted (the stones underlapping each other as the structure closed towards the top) and a substantial flagstone which lies nearby would have capped it. When this grave was excavated in 1952 archaeologists found much food for thought. Inside the chamber, the surface of a carefully laid pavement revealed the imprint of a body that had been buried in the crouched position. At one point between the stones they found a cobbled area; no one could do more than guess at its purpose. And large quantities of quartz fragments had been broadcast, like fertiliser, over the kerbs and deep core of the cairn. The presence of this broken rock is a recurring feature in neolithic tomb building. Visually quartzite is a singular rock, of virgin whiteness and beautifully grained. It sits in patches on the summer mountains like a memory of snow. Ley lines are said to meet where quartz-rich rocks are found. Its crystals can be caused to throb, like tiny hearts, with uncanny regularity. It has a strong hint of life within it to which, who knows, those fresh, uncluttered neolithic minds might well have been receptive. Why else should they have sprinkled it so liberally around the places of their dead?

Carn Daly. Was this the Druid's circle?

Much nearer to Loch Ness, above the village of Milton, is another chambered cairn. It is less impressive than its much better known near neighbour; unexcavated, with a single thorn tree growing in its centre, it hides any secrets it may hold under a tight covering of rank field grass. Yet here speculations on the nature of its prehistory mix with legend. And the legend is a weighty one, worth the telling.

Once upon a time a Druid lived here, or hereabouts. There was, in fancy, no Loch Ness then, only a dry valley, verdant and fair, surrounded by slopes of oak and birch. It supported a decent population who had long known the secret of peaceful coexistence. The men spent their days in fishing the deep, slow-moving river that ran through the valley, hunting the fierce boar in the forest and the deer on the mountain, and tending the fat cattle in their fields. Their women talked happily together, spun wool and brought up healthy and uninhibited children.

Daly the Druid was spiritual father to these people. I expect that he would have been grave and severe, using his mystic forces to control his big, obedient family. He was a practical magician. The act for which he will always be remembered was the blessing of a well that lay in the valley floor which thereafter gave water with rare medicinal qualities. Few illnesses were able to resist its tonic effect though, given the general good health of the people and the Druid's draconian rule, it was probably both easy and prudent to make a quick recovery. Daly was also thrifty and he did

Corrimony passage grave

not care to see his very special water running to waste, so he fashioned a stone to cap the well when not in use. Then he issued a strongly worded edict: 'Be sure to re-place the stone upon my well after drawing water from it, or great destruction and misery will befall you all.'

One fateful day years later a woman of the valley took her beaker to the well. She was drowsy in the heat of the day and had almost forgotten that she had left her unruly male child unattended in her thatched stone house. Suddenly she heard a neighbour's urgent shout; the child was playing close to the red embers of her cook-ing fire. She ran, forgetting her beaker, the uncapped well and the Druid's clear instruction. When, having snatched her boy from harm's way, she returned, it was too late. The well was gushing water like a severed artery and the pond around it was already many feet deep. The strongest swimmer in the community was unable to reach the well or find its stone cap in the swirl.

As the days went by all that fair valley was inundated. Anything that could not run or swim disappeared beneath the all-consuming flood. Men, women, children and cattle scrambled up the hillsides in unaccustomed confusion and fast-growing misery. Daly watched the chaotic scene from the safety of his circle with a saturnine grin. And so Loch Ness was formed out of a moment's forgetfulness, and the people cried: *Tha loch 'nis ann* which means, there's a loch there now. This is one story of how the great water came by its name.

Three miles north-east of Dores, on General Wade's road built in 1732 from

Johnson's and Boswell's circle

Inverness to Fort Augustus, is a chambered cairn that attracted the attention of that dogmatic man of letters, Samuel Johnson. On a fine late August morning in 1773 the doctor was ready, as usual, with the dismissive comment. He observed, 'that to go and see one is only to see that it is nothing, for there is neither art nor power in it, and seeing one is as much as one would wish'. Boswell, however, took time to notice that 'There was a double circle of stones, one of very large ones and one of smaller ones', and described it as a 'Druid's temple'.

On Essich Moor, two miles east of Boswell's 'druid temple' and on a high slope, is a fine example of a Long Cairn. These structures, also known as tumuli, are elongated mounds of stone or earth which often cover more than a single chamber. This one is almost 400 feet long and roofs three separate rectangular compartments. Evidence suggests that it is later than the units it encloses.

One can only guess at the exact purpose of these cairns and circles. So much change has taken place since the first stones were raised five thousand years ago.

The original structures were certainly altered by successive builders; the cairns were denuded for use in field walls; grave robbers and ghoulish trophy hunters took their pick of the contents of the exposed chambers, though, where the soil was acid, not much would have been left; zealous farmers of the last two centuries removed what they could of the buildings to simplify their ploughing. The stones themselves, solid, even aggressive, are speechless. Apart from them, all we have are some burnt bones, some ash and traces of the cremating charcoal; a sprinkling of magic quartz pebbles; perhaps a flint arrowhead; cupmarks, round holes ground out by abrasive stones, in the walls of passages and chambers and over ring cairns.

While neolithic sites are scarce around Loch Ness it has its share of Iron Age duns and forts. The fact that to fulfil their function as defensive structures they had to be sited on ridges or narrow hilltops unsuitable for farming or modern building has largely preserved them from damage. These 'family units' (as they might be called in this age of bureaucratic terminology) can be divided roughly into three categories – the timber-laced Fort, the Stone Fort and the Dun. The distinction between the last two is one of size; I understand that to qualify as a Fort the building should have an internal area of more than 1300 sq. m. The Dun may be as small as 350 sq. m., suitable for a single family. The Fort might have been home to more than one, or simply a mansion appropriate to a powerful chief.

It is thought that these buildings were not used for continuous occupation. For the most part their situations are remote, exposed and daunting. They were places to retreat to in time of attack, rather like communal air-raid shelters, and their Iron Age owner/builders lived nearby, on lower, more comfortable ground, in hut circles. One would imagine that a lookout may have been permanently employed for these airy sites commanded excellent views, and the times were tense. There was keen competition for arable land, and, I expect, for pretty women, good cattle, jewellery and even for the forts themselves. It is unlikely that human nature was any different then and what laws there were favoured the hard man.

At least four Iron Age forts overlook Loch Ness, each substantial and built on carefully selected sites. Dun Scripan stands high on the south-west side of the Loch at the end of the hill road that links the settlement of Grotaig with Lewiston village. Created on a prominent fold of the hillside, it commands a fine view of the Loch and the local terrain to the north and east but its situation lacks the natural defences of the neighbouring Dun Dearduil, right across the Loch. This stylish and dramatic looking little mountain, only around 250 m. high, must have delighted the heart of the Iron Age military architect. Its narrow summit, encircled on all sides by steep or precipitous ground, provides a birds's-eye view in every direction. On the north and east the glacial gouged gorge of the River Farigaig, difficult to cross in any but the driest conditions, takes the form of an immaculate moat. Even the more gently sloping ground towards Stratherrick is abruptly nicked, immediately below the dun, by an overhanging cliff from which boulders could readily be hurled at aspiring invaders. The collapsed walls of the fort, decoratively buried under turf and bright green moss, contain a roughly oblong concavity.

Dun Riach, a little withdrawn from the Loch on Ashie Moor, is less exciting from a defensive point of view in that it has only one impregnable side – a fifty-foot vertical cliff – on the south, but it still must have been an effective strongpoint. Though of small elevation it dominates a widish area of flat, boggy moor and is thought to have served as a fortified retreat for the hutted communities in the nearby area.

The last of our four major Iron Age forts lies partly concealed below a much later building, the ruinous Urquhart Castle. It is obvious that the defensible nature of this site – a strong promontory partly surrounded by water and narrowly connected to the land – has made it attractive to successive generations. Its Iron Age connections are manifest in rocks fused together around the foundations of the present pile. This significant feature, known as vitrification, can also be found on Dun Dearduil. Our other two forts are non-vitrified. It was once believed to be the result of volcanism but in 1777 the archaeologist John Williams, excavating a site above

Vitrified rocks, fused together by chance or design?

31

Strathpeffer, formed the opinion that man had used heat to weld stones into a single solid mass. The walls of forts in which vitrification can be found are always of the timber-laced type – a wooden frame within two dry stone walls. Ignition of the timber, by whatever cause, in a ventilated but enclosed space ultimately made charcoal. The steady, intense heat of burning charcoal produces chemical changes in other substances. Over a thousand years before these forts were built, men of the Near East had been smelting iron by its use.

Did this condition come about by chance, or by design? Opinion is divided. Some say that enemy action, domestic carelessness, forest or grass fires caused the timber lacing of the forts to ignite. Of course this is possible. But timber struts, separated and probably damp, would have been slow to catch and, except in the case of an attack, the fire would have been quickly put out. Those who favour the 'chance' theory trace the rising flames as they lap stones high in the walls and cause them to shatter and fall back into the furnace beneath. This would certainly create conditions suitable for the production of charcoal, and subsequent melting of the stones *if the stones were of fusible rock, such as schist.* But almost all the forts and duns in our general area are built in sandstone country, of local rock, and sandstone is unsuitable for fusing. One cannot see Iron Age workers searching far and wide for schists simply to add a little variety to their building. Another thing is, if it were by chance agency, why did *so many* forts catch fire and burn with such ferocity?

I myself incline to the idea (since I am no authority on the matter I won't use the word 'theory') that vitrification was a planned attempt to give extra strength to the walls of forts at, and just above, foundation level, and that Stone Age builders deemed it of sufficient importance to merit collecting 'melting' stones even from considerable distances. It might have been done when the walls were still low by feeding the fire with great quantities of timber (probably birch) and capping it with flat slabs, thus creating a charcoal burner's pit, or kiln. It is said that Caesar saw it done in Gaul. Is there any reason why it should not have been done here?

While the waspish magician Daly gave his name to a chambered cairn, a beautiful woman gave hers to one of our four Iron Age forts. To set Deirdre and Uisnach's three lusty sons on the narrow top of Dun Dearduil (which translates as Deirdre's Fort) may sound like a piece of romantic manipulation but legend is the child of a casual affair between fact and fiction, and none the worse for it. The beginnings of this sad tale are too well known to need inclusion here but is said that after Naisi had fallen in love with Deirdre, who was the King's intended bride, they fled, with his two brothers, from Ulster and the wrath of the obsessed Concobar. They travelled northeast, supported by a few followers, through the stone hills of Loch Etive to the long valley of the 'Black Loch' until they found a place which, because it was both impregnable and a perfect watchtower, would bring them comfort and buy them some time. Perhaps already there was a fort there, empty and ripe for occupancy, and soon the brothers and their attendants would have been engaged in home improvements, consolidating the walls – already vitrified, who knows? – and roofing the structure with hides and turf. So we may think of them – the magnificent Naisi and his brothers, all Knights of the Red Branch, and the harper's exquisite daughter, beloved of Naisi, setting up house on the tip of this crag. From its secure vantage point they could sally forth to fish and hunt, and when that was done the two lovers might enjoy their love, perilous and star-crossed as it was. But in the wind, loud with ravens and wild with drifting hawks, they must have heard the angry tones of Concobar, robbed of the woman he had chosen by his own cousin, and burning for revenge.

Deirdre's fort and the 'Black Loch'

Let us further imagine how the brothers came to extend their forage, crossing the Loch in their coracles and hunting on the high moors to the north. Adventurous spirits crave excitement, warriors denied war become ill-at-ease and restless; soon the trio fell to stealing cattle, to the fury of the men of Alba who soon wished to be rid of them. With rather unknightly expedience the brothers approached the King of Alba, offering warrior service in exchange for the King's protection. Their offer was accepted, but it led to a fresh danger; rumour of Deirdre's fatal beauty reached this second king who, like Concobar, wished to possess her. She, steadfast to Naisi, would have none of him and so Alba, like David in the Bible, placed Naisi in the forefront of every battle. Yet he triumphed over all the odds, and his brothers with him, until Alba, quite out of patience, told his own men to make a quick end of them. Deirdre, more cautious and intuitive than her lover, sensed the danger and they retraced their steps to Argyle. There they dwelt for a while at Loch Etive, but that is another story. They never returned to the 'Black Loch'.

Perhaps it is all true; at any rate, it ought to be. And I have another string to add to my bow. On the south of Glenurquhart there is a hill called Carn Magsna, a low ridge shaggy with heather and patched with cold grey slab. Nowadays it is all but submerged beneath a green sea of forestry plantings but it can never have been a conspicuous hill, just an excrescence rising like a wart on the skin of a pulpy, peaty moor. From its indefinite top the little green platform, where Deirdre's fort once stood, can be seen clearly, five miles away, over Loch Ness. The punchline is that Carn Magsna means 'the rocky hill of the Sons of Uisnach'. It is nice to imagine that, one winter's day over two thousand years ago, a tall, fresh-faced, muscular young man caught a glimpse of his distant dwelling, thought of his love, and said to his brothers, 'I've had enough of hunting for today. Let's go home!'.

The Picts, a small, swarthy, marauding people, probably of Celtic origin, occupied much of north-east Scotland from the third century A.D. onwards. Place names of Pictish origin can be found around the Loch. This numerous and vigorous new race absorbed the old inhabitants by force of numbers, and Inverness became the capital of Northern Pictland. It was to visit their king, Brude, that Columba, an Irish prince and priest (fresh from the founding of his monastery on Iona), made his way up the Great Glen in 565 A.D. At first he was received with suspicion. There had been a battle between the Picts and the Dalriad Scots, with whom Columba had common blood, and the Scots had been defeated. But Columba was a Christian, with the power to work miracles. At Brude's stronghold, situated, as legend has it, on top of Craig Phadraig, above Inverness, an undoubted Iron Age fort, Columba was rudely confronted by a locked gate, but its bolts could not resist the sign of the cross. They sprang open to allow the visitor to enter, to the king's amazement and alarm. From that moment onwards Brude treated Columba with growing deference and honour.

Columba, no doubt, did many deeds of charity by stealth but he would also have realised the need for some more ostentatious displays of his power. He was there, after all, to convert the pagan Picts, to wean them from the influence of their own priests. A chance to show the efficacy of his faith to an alien audience (as at the king's locked gate) came one day when he was visiting Lochend, near where the River Ness begins. He met a party of Picts who had just buried a companion; they told Columba that the poor fellow had been mauled to death by a water monster. Touched by compassion but properly aware of his own value to the Church, he instructed a companion named Mocumin to swim the river and commandeer a boat moored on the opposite bank. Mocumin did so. Inevitably the Beast, having just tasted blood, broke the surface and made for him, and was within snapping distance when the saint raised an admonitory hand and told it to stop. The beast swam off, with undulating humps and bellowing most frightfully, while Mocumin, trembling with fear and cold, returned to his master. It was indeed a famous miracle and one which seekers after the True Monster, 1400 years later, would give their souls to see re-enacted.

On this and a subsequent visit to Loch Ness-side Columba was ever zealous in promoting the faith. His biographer, St Adamnan, writing from hearsay in the next century, gives glowing reports of his activities in his Life of Saint Columba. A dominant theme is the fierce conflict between his hero and the Pictish priests, a war of attrition with the souls of the people as the booty. When, for instance, Columba and his brethren were once singing vespers outside King Brude's royal house, the druids tried to shout him down, but the saint was instantly supplied with such a strong voice that his roared-out rendition of the forty-fifth psalm struck terror into all who were present, including the king. By then, indeed, Brude had a healthy respect for the crusading Christian which was to ripen into affection as the years went by, and which was reciprocated. At another time word reached Columba of a Loch-side spring that was so poisonous that the Picts worshipped it as a god. This idolatry shocked the saint and he visited the polluted water without delay. The druid magicians smirked balefully, hoping that he would drink, but Columba, with a single blessing, rendered the water not only wholesome but therapeutic.

Columba's main adversary was the chief druid, Broichan, who continued to resist his teaching even after the king had come to terms with it. Only the fact that he was Brude's foster-father permitted the druid such dissent from royal policy. On one occasion Columba demanded that Broichan should set free an Irish slave girl, and when this was refused Columba hinted that the druid would die. Soon, indeed, Broichan was at death's door but the king interceded with Columba on his behalf. A deal was struck; a slave girl's freedom for a chief druid's life. When the girl was set at liberty Columba cured his adversary by touching him with a magic white pebble which he had taken from the River Ness. Formed of quartzite, I'm sure, but this pebble was unique; it could float in water 'like an apple or a nut' and effected instant cures.

One may imagine that Broichan had very mixed feelings about this blackmail, and he continued to annoy and oppose the saint at every turn. When Columba wanted to leave Loch Ness and return to Argyle his enemy called upon the God of the Elements to send dense mist and a gale from the south-west. This dismal forecast failed to dismay the saint who knelt in prayer as his sails were being set. His boat at once drove steadily into the gale which then died away, soon to return from the opposite quarter.

There is a single account of Columba paying a private visit. As he walked by the Loch in the quiet evening the Holy Ghost spoke to him, saying that nearby lived a heathen of great natural goodness, now close to death. The saint went quickly to his house to carry out an urgent baptism; the dying man was baptised and all his family with him. This account is the more interesting as Adamnan, usually chary of giving locations, tells us that the baptism took place in a district called Airchartdan, which today is known as Urquhart. It is possible that Columba founded the church

Reconstruction of a crannog (see p. 123).

at Invermoriston and legend suggests that the well nearby is that which he purified to the druids' discomfiture.

Certainly Columba was a great saint, energetic, pious, filled to the brim with missionary zeal, but he owes much of his reputation to a fine biographer. Thus he overshadows the ministry of two other saints who preceded him by one hundred and fifty years. The names of St. Ninian and St. Drostan are ubiquitously recorded in this glen and Drostan is, in fact, its patron saint. Ancient records tell us that his relics lay in St. Ninian's Temple (its site is just east of Drumnadrochit on the Inverness road) until Reformation times. But without such a hagiographer as Adamnan to guide us we know little of the doings of these early saints. We may think, however, that their teaching lacked Columba's convincing punch for by the time he came on the scene the Picts had evidently lapsed back into paganism. After Columba the Christian church appears to have been quite strongly established in the region.

Our view of the history of the next few hundred years can be compared to shafts of pale moonlight in a night of scudding clouds. Sometimes an amorphous shape will form in the shadows; it is gone before it can be grasped. Legend and fact fight for equal recognition, osmosing with each other in the process. Our best marker of time and events is Castle Urquhart and its headland site on which once rested the iron age fort and associated hut dwellings. For centuries the castle has been the Loch's most prominent single man-made feature, and a place which has attracted events, both shadowy and substantial, like a lodestone.

In or about 1160 A.D. Castle Urquhart, probably then a timbered earthwork (or motehill), was given to an Irish mercenary knight, Conachar Mor Mac Aoidh, by King David I. This Conachar (not to be confused with Deirdre's royal suitor of much earlier times, who was Conachar Mac Nessa, otherwise Concobar) had given the king service in the recent war and Urquhart was his reward. It is said that he was a mighty warrior, as were many of his kind out of Ulster, and he was prolific too; from his ample loins sprang the Mackays, the Forbeses and, not unexpectedly, the Urquharts who took their name from his glen.

A boar's head, common to the arms of these three families, recalls a deed for which Conachar does not deserve full credit. For some years he had owned a dog, once of great strength and stature, known plainly as 'Big Dog' from the Gaelic, *An Cu Mor*. Big Dog was old now. His eyes were becoming opaque, his coat was as scuffed as a worn carpet and his hind quarters had grown stiff. He spent his days in wandering round the castle, looking lost. When he met his master all he could do was to raise his ears questioning and stir his thick tail.

I would like to think that it was compassion for his old companion of the hunt that made Conachar decide to have Big Dog put down. It was fortunate for him that his command was overheard by an old woman who had the 'second sight'. 'Let the dog live', she said, 'his own day awaits him.' To this Conachar agreed, and on a day when he set forth to rid the countryside of a most furious and savage boar Big Dog sprang to his feet, in the manner of his youth, and followed him. The boar was found in its lair, and a long and bloody encounter followed. Try as he might Conachar could not penetrate the beast's thick, bristly hide with his sword. He was repeatedly gored by its sharp tusks. It seemed all up with him when Big Dog uttered a tremendous bark, joined the fray and tore the boar's throat open with his teeth.

But Big Dog did not survive his day. In killing the boar he had received a mortal wound. Conachar lived on as the master of Castle Urquhart for many years and when he died he was buried, so legend has it, with his sword beneath a great boulder, which has ever since been known as Clach Ochonachair (Conachar's Stone). Nobody knows where Big Dog is buried.

3 Capturing the Castle

W E MUST stay with Castle Urquhart; it is central to the mediaeval and early modern history of the Loch. While events in other parts of the area are mostly conjectural those at Urquhart are precisely documented. During these centuries the sandstone point, so obviously suited to its purpose, has seen the growth of buildings from primitive Iron Age fort to a sophisticated and effective military complex. The first major work, of which massive evidence still remains, was the building, in the 13th century, of an interior defensive wall and the heavily fortified central tower. It is likely that the ditch, a feature which would have existed from the days of the timber-laced fort, was dug more deeply at around this period.

In 1296, after the battle of Dunbar, Edward I of England hurried north to complete his victory over the Scots. From Elgin he sent detachments to secure various castles and fortified places, of which Urquhart was one. Sir William Fitzwarine, an English knight, became its first keeper.

If Edward thought the Scots would be knocked out by the first blow of his hammer he was mistaken. Wallace rose against him in the South while Andrew Moray, son of a local landowner, moved against, among other places, Castle Urquhart. Fitzwarine was soon in trouble. On a certain Sunday in 1297 he travelled to Inverness to discuss the situation with Sir Reginald le Chen, the English commander there. During his return to Urquhart he was set upon by Moray and an Inverness burgess, Alex Pilche, and lost several men and horses. The skirmish is thought to have taken place above Dochfour, on the old hill road to Drumnadrochit. In those days there was no road along the north-east shore of the Loch.

Loch Ness

Fitzwarine managed to reach the castle safely, but he was a worried man. The Countess of Ross, wishing to keep in favour with Edward who had held her husband prisoner since Dunbar, turned up the next morning with her son's army, and an offer to help; but the constable, suspicious and distrustful, turned it down. In spite of his hesitation, she gave him considerable assistance, but even so Moray gathered a large force and, in a night attack, several of the defenders were killed, including Fitzwarine's son.

Edward was not unaware of this insurrection. In June he wrote to Henry le Chen, the 'warrior-bishop' of Aberdeen, with instructions to relieve the besieged garrison. Accordingly le Chen, with an earl and two knights, at the head of a body of men, set out towards Urquhart. At Inverness they met the Countess of Ross and John of the Aird whose son, like the countess' husband, was still Edward's prisoner. Both were only too ready to help them for their own very good reasons. When Andrew Moray and his patriots heard of the approach of a considerable army they slunk

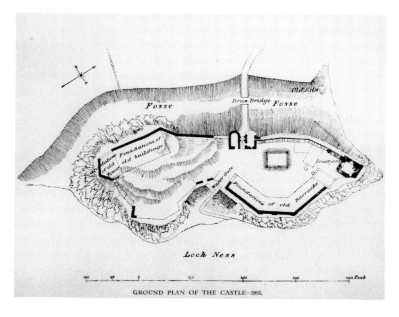

GROUND PLAN OF THE CASTLE—1893.

Urquhart Castle 'in the olden time'

41

away into the hills and woods, following the age-old strategy of 'wait and see', for it was known that Sir William Wallace was on the march at the head of experienced troops. Moray's withdrawal and the arrival of le Chen's army gave Fitzwarine time and resources to construct massive towers at the landward entrance and to improve other fortifications. This work, by an ironic twist of fate, was to bring more comfort to the Scots than to the English.

Wallace was now moving steadily north. From Aberdeen he marched westward; to Cromarty, perhaps to Moray's nearby castle; even, perhaps, to Urquhart itself. At any rate by the end of that year the English had gone and the keeper of the castle was Sir Alexander Forbes – a fitting appointment for the great-great-grandson of Conachar (see p. 37).

The war went on indecisively for some years. Eventually Edward lost all patience with the situation. Reassured by a treaty with France, he invaded Scotland at the head of a large army, partly mercenary, and marched, almost unopposed, as far as the castle of Lochindorb in Morayshire. Consolidated at this stronghold he sent his detachments to subdue the towns and fortresses of the north with clear instructions to treat any resistance with the utmost severity. In many places his stern reputation was sufficient, but the stone castle of Urquhart, so recently fortified by English money and labour, proved a hard nut to crack. Alexander Forbes, no doubt the more determined by reason of his family's earlier association with the castle, rejected a call to surrender and a prolonged siege began. Edward returned to the south leaving his army on the neck of land between the castle and the steep Creag na h-Iolaire (Eagle's Rock) to starve the defenders into submission.

When, at last, their food was finished Forbes decided to risk all and attempt to break out. But first he took steps to protect his dynasty. His pregnant wife, disguised as a peasant, was allowed through the circle of besieging English. It is said that from the crags above she was able to witness the last act of the drama as her husband and his men went out to certain death. Lady Forbes escaped to Ireland, where her son was born.

Edward gave Urquhart Castle into the custodial hands of Sir Alexander Cumming who held it until 1306 when Robert Bruce was crowned king of Scotland and the English were once more ejected. Seven years later King Robert created his loyal nephew Thomas Randolph Earl of Moray, which province included Urquhart and Glenmoriston. Later the castle and its lands were claimed by the young Alexander Forbes who had returned from Ireland. King Robert would not withdraw the gift from his nephew but gave Forbes substantial lands in Mar.

Edward Baliol, son of John Baliol who had ruled Scotland between 1292–96, had been after the crown of Scotland for some time, and now Edward III of England came up with open military support. Ruinous war once again engulfed Scotland and for a while Baliol's star seemed in the ascendant but eventually he was driven back across the border. During this invasion five Scottish castles kept their doors stoutly closed: Dumbarton, Lochleven, Kildrummie, Lochmaben – and Urquhart. Sir Robert Lauder, its current constable, held it secure again in 1335 after Edward III had mounted yet another expedition in Baliol's support. Sir Robert was a man of many virtues, pious, just, brave and a true patriot. He also kept a good table, and entertained lavishly. On the 4th July 1342 a party at the Castle included knights, earls and bishops 'and many others, clergymen and laymen'. His daughter Anne, who had married into the Chisholm family, had a son called Robert, and this boy lived with his grandfather for many years. He became constable of the castle, in succession to his grandfather, in 1359.

In the next three hundred years the castle changed hands many times. It was closely associated with strong men, weak men, good men and some very bad men, of whom the Earl of Buchan, better known as 'The Wolf', was certainly the worst. As Sir Robert Chisholm grew older he gave up his lands in the parish before resigning his position as keeper of the Castle in 1390. Buchan, second son of the ruling king, Robert II, acquired these lands outright, and from his brother, the Earl of Stratherne, a lease of the rest of the barony. Buchan began by refusing to pay the rent or give up the lease. Stratherne complained to his father, and the King mediated gently, but Buchan continued unabashed. By now he had fallen into very bad ways, terrorising the countryside with fire and sword, soon becoming known as the Wolf of Badenoch. He married, for territorial gain, the widowed Countess of Ross, and was immediately unfaithful to her with a woman of her household. The countess, treated with the utmost cruelty, fled from her home and brought her sorry

The Wolf of
Badenoch

43

situation to the notice of the Bishops of Moray and Ross. In their judgement Buchan was told to send away his mistress and restore all appropriate rights to his wife; and to provide sureties for his good behaviour. This last Buchan did, invoking the name of Thomas Chisholm, constable of the castle, as one of his guarantors. Chisholm, along with two other 'great and noble persons' agreed to pay a penalty of £200 each time Buchan reneged on the agreement.

The insolent and untrustworthy earl let them all down. He retained his mistress, continued to dishonour his wife and took a violent spite against the Bishop of Moray. He robbed churches, for which crime he was excommunicated. This so inflamed his psychopathic personality that in 1390 – the year of the king's death – he led his henchmen to Forres and burned the town to the ground. The following month he attacked Elgin, destroying St. Giles's church and the rich houses of church dignitaries before venting his fury on 'the noble and beautiful cathedral of Moray' with all its irreplaceable contents. This time he had gone too far. Public opinion was outraged and the gloved iron fist of the Church finally subdued him. Having done abject penance he was absolved on the promise of making some sort of reparation for the massive injury he had inflicted on church and people.

He died quietly in his bed but he had fostered evil. His two bastard sons had inherited his violent behaviour and the Earldom of Ross (which he had acquired through his marriage, and which now included Urquhart and Glenmoriston) was the subject of complicated and vicious dispute. In the interests of brevity I shall simply mention that by 1398 our castle was under the 'protection' of Alexander the Crafty (Keppoch), brother of Donald, Lord of the Isles, who had put in his loyal supporter Charles Maclean as its constable. Maclean married a daughter of a Glenurquhart family, the Cummings.

The unscrupulous Regent of Scotland, Albany, persisted in a claim to the Earldom of Ross, but Donald of the Isles had even greater ambitions. He intended to supplant Albany and then take the Stewart crown of Scotland for his own. He raised a considerable army, including contingents from Urquhart, at Inverness and marched south, but not before he had sacked the village of Muir of Ord because it had received him without much enthusiasm. Tempers were easily frayed in those days. At Harlaw, in Aberdeenshire, he was confronted by an army led by none other than the Wolf's son Alex. They were cousins with connections by marriage and they fought each other, with a special ferocity, to a standstill. Donald of the Isles went home. Alex, a true son of his father, snatched Urquhart and Glenmoriston from under his Regent uncle's nose and held on to them. When the Regent died his son, Duke Murdoch, entered into an agreement with Alexander (who, like his father before him, had contracted a loveless marriage with a widowed countess, in this case Lady Mar) to the effect that Alexander should manage the Earldom of Urquhart and Glenmoriston, and that they would share the revenues on a fifty-fifty basis. It all worked out very badly for Murdoch. When James I returned from captivity in England he was much angered by the truculence and lawlessness of his nobles; he determined to make some examples. The luckless Duke Murdoch and his two sons were arrested on a vague charge, tried, found guilty and executed in Stirling in 1425. It comes as no surprise to learn that Alex, Earl of Mar, was a member of the jury who condemned him.

Even the king was not above such double dealing. From Inverness he summoned Alexander, son of Donald, the new Lord of the Isles, and a number of chiefs to meet with him. No sooner had they gathered than James's soldiery overcame and imprisoned them. The king, it is said, was delighted at the success of his stratagem, and, in triumphant mood, sent several lords to the executioner forthwith. Alexander was set free after making the necessary promises but he did not forget this treacherous act. He made a petulant attack on Inverness and adjoining crown lands, setting part of that town on fire. The king led an army to put down this dis-order, and Alexander was imprisoned, but his uncle Keppoch supported his cause and gave the king's forces, under Mar and Caithness, a bloody beating at Inver-lochy.

Mar was badly wounded, but he survived that battle. When he died in 1435 Urquhart and Glenmoriston once again became crown property. The king's violent death in 1437 gave Alexander of the Isles (on whom the title of Earl of Ross had earlier been conferred) a chance to slip in and establish possession. He installed Hector Buie, son of the former constable Charles Maclean, in that function.

During a short intermission in chronic civil war the profitable business of cattle stealing became popular. Repeated raids from Lochaber reivers on the fat stock of Urquhart and its neighbouring parish infuriated Hector Buie, now a powerful man locally. He decided that the Camerons must be taught a lesson and accordingly went into Lochaber for an orgy of indiscriminate killing and stealing. Lochiel, the Camerons' chief, hurried back from a visit to Ireland but Hector had already taken important hostages whom he held in the old Castle of Bona at Lochend, and when Lochiel arrived Hector threatened to kill them. Lochiel offered an exchange – he had two of Hector's sons, and a number of Glenurquhart men. Maclean declined, and a multiple hanging took place. The old Castle of Bona, grossly disturbed during the cutting of the Caledonian Canal, is now a scanty ruin, but for many years it shuddered to the ghostly cries of these innocent victims.

Hector probably died at Bona, but the next keeper of Castle Urquhart was Thomas Ogilvy of Balfour who held the appointment until 1452. Alexander of the Isles (also Earl of Ross), was dead by then, and his son John had quarrelled with the king, James II. The king, as was often customary, had chosen a wife for the young earl but soon after the marriage the bride's father, Sir James Livingston, had been judged treacherous. Because of this the king refused to pay the promised settlement, and John, a hot-headed youth, expressed his protest by taking Castle Urquhart (then Crown property) and for good measure firing the stronghold of Ruthven, in Badenoch. He was simply too powerful for Parliament to control and before very long he was in possession of the barony for his lifetime at the rental of £100 per annum. Thereafter John supported James II loyally, and when James was killed by an exploding cannon in 1460, he paid lip service to the dead king's young son. But he was a man of unlimited ambition which was revealed the following year when he was secretly in touch with Edward IV of England and the banished Earl of Douglas. His astounding proposal was that he, along with a veteran soldier named Donald Balloch, and Donald's son, John, should become mercenaries of England, and if, with Edward's help, Scotland was conquered, all the land north of the Forth was to be partitioned between the two Earls and the Ballochs. This unusual treaty was concluded in 1462 and John of the Isles went into action without delay. He raised the north but his splendid insurrection went off like a damp squib. His troops melted away and he came to the young king, cap in hand. James III was merciful until, in 1474, John's treasonable association with Edward came to light. Parliament commanded him to attend but he disregarded the instruction; he was branded a traitor and his estates were under threat of forfeiture. A force was assembled to implement the sentence but before it moved north the Earl prudently approached the King and a compromise was achieved. Considering his atrocious treachery one feels that John of the Isles came rather well out of it. He was allowed to keep most of his lands and his ancient title was confirmed by parliament, but the Earldom of Ross was once again vested in the Crown. George, Earl of Huntly, became the new constable of the castle.

And with that the eighty-year reign of the Island Chiefs over Loch Ness came to an end. As is invariable, the power plays of the leaders brought only misery and confusion to the common people. Their allegiances were torn this way and that. The crown lost revenue through unpaid rents. It was not, in fact, a felicitous time for anybody.

Ewen Maclean, one of the three sons of Hector Buie Maclean, who had died at the hostage killing at Bona, had no rights in Urquhart and Moriston now that Islesmen were gone, but spent the next thirty years trying to unseat the sub-tenant of the barony, Hugh Rose, Baron Kilravock. Hugh Rose was eventually heartily sick of Urquhart and the trouble his appointment had caused him. He asked Huntly to relieve him of it. His request was granted in 1482, and Sir Duncan Grant, Knight of Freuchie, was asked to fill the vacancy.

Sir Duncan's family had owned Stratherrick on the east side of Loch Ness from the 13th century until 1420. They might have held some of it even longer had it not been for the misbehaviour of one of their members. Gruer Mor of Port Clair was newly married, and his young wife was visiting her friends and receiving nuptial

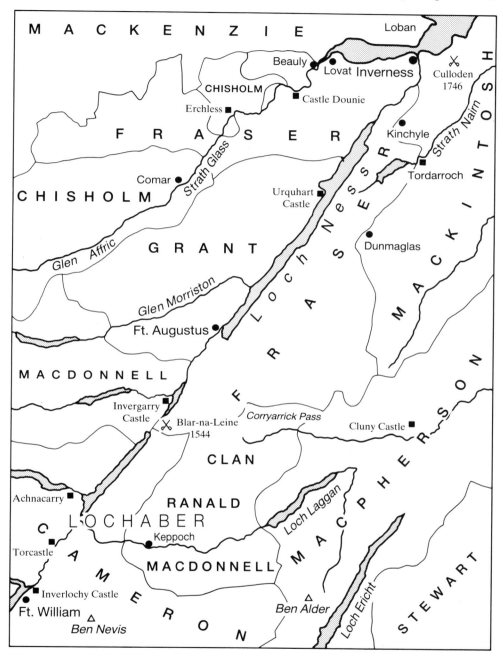

The Clans around Loch Ness

Castle Urquhart in more peaceful times, the 1930s, with The Gondolier *paddle steamer*

gifts. Laurence Grant of Foyers (which was the Grants' last possession in Stratherrick) was, I shouldn't wonder, a young man who had a hot glance and an insolent tongue. There is no record of what he said to the lady when she came to Foyers on that fatal day but she thought herself insulted, and told her husband so. Gruer Mor would not stand for it; he manned his galleys and set out for Foyers. Grant rowed out on the Loch to meet him. There was a savage fight in the Viking tradition; bodies were washed up afterwards in a bay west of Foyers whose name commemorates the event. The Grants were beaten and Laurence was forced onto the hostile north-east shore. Here, on a steep slope called Ruiskich, Gruer caught up and killed him. With the insult to his wife avenged the victor regrouped his men, returned to Foyers and promptly annexed it. There is a certain no-nonsense quality about this tale that cannot fail to please all but the most fastidious.

Although Sir Duncan had been appointed the new constable of Castle Urquhart he was too old to take an active role in the arduous tasks of restoring law and order in the barony. He delegated these duties to his grandson John, also known as the Red Bard, who took over from Kilravock without delay. There was much to do. The Clan 'Ic Uian, who had strongly supported Ewen Maclean, resisted the incomer furiously and performed acts of sabotage for which they were made memorable in song and story. In Glenmoriston the Macdonalds also opposed the Grants, so that the Red Bard had, in effect, to fight a war on two fronts. But he persevered, and as the years went by his reputation for prudence, pacification and even-handed justice spread well beyond the bounds of the barony. He was the King's man, and the King rewarded his loyalty in 1509 by making him an outright gift of Urquhart and Glenmoriston. There follows a peaceful intermission in the turbulent history of Loch Ness-side.

But only until 1513. The death of the popular James IV at Flodden sparked off new confusions and old aspirations. The Islesmen were on the move again. Sir Donald Macdonald of Lochalsh, newly proclaimed Lord of the Isles, brought an army to Urquhart, sacked the castle and laid waste the glen. The castle was stripped of all its contents. For three years Sir Donald maintained a large foothold in the parish, encouraged by the Clan 'Ic Uian and the Macdonalds in Glenmoriston. Eventually the Grants dislodged him and in 1517 the Red Bard brought a civil action against Sir Donald and his accomplices for the loss and damage incurred by their invasion of his property. He obtained judgement in the sum of £2000. It is unlikely that this debt was ever recovered.

The prudent Bard, determined to avoid any further occupation by hostile clans, invited the Captain of Clan Cameron to enter into a bond of friendship and mutual aid. The treaty was signed in Castle Urquhart in 1520 before some powerful and influential people. Young Donald Cameron and Miss Agnes Grant were to provide a touch of practical romance. Their marriage was to begin with a handshake and be followed by an immediate bedding. A proper Church wedding would follow, as soon as some Papal difficulty was solved. And the whole arrangement was given an unqualified blessing by the vicar of Kilmonivaig.

When the Red Bard died, in 1528, he left the barony and estates to his son, Seumas who, quite unlike his father, was something of a rogue. When James V decided that because of their incessant trouble-making it was necessary to exterminate the militant males of Clan Chattan, he called upon some Highland chiefs, including Seumas, to perform this draconian act. Seumas hesitated and then secretly supported the rebels in a dastardly attack upon the Daviot castle of Ogilvy of Strathnairn; several men of Urquhart were also concerned in it. A tax on crime – by which some offenses would be pardoned on a payment being made to the Crown – was known as *composition*, and Seumas bought himself and his men complete freedom from prosecution for a crime which was in the order of high treason. Not only that, but in that same year of 1535 the king granted him and the inhabitants of Urquhart exemption from the judgement of all regional courts. This license for lawlessness led to a state of near anarchy in the glen.

Nine years later Seumas, the Laird of Grant, joined Lord Lovat and the Earl of Huntly in an expedition aimed at putting down disturbances, and supporting Ranald Gallda – related to the Grants through marriage – against John of Moidart in a claim for the leadership of Clan Ranald. The Macdonalds of Glengarry and Keppoch and the Camerons were for John, and it was into their country that Huntly, Lovat and Seumas marched against an invisible enemy. Disappointed, relaxed and unwatchful they turned for home, and at the Water of Gloy their armies went their separate ways. Huntly and Grant, with most of the troops, made for Strathspey. Lovat, Ronald Gallda, the Frasers and the Urquhart and Glenmoriston men followed the Great Glen.

The insurgents had underestimated the wily John of Moidart. Hidden in the dense forests on the north of Loch Lochy he was able to observe the split-up of their forces at Spean Bridge. Like a cat stalking a mouse he matched his opponents' pace as they moved unsuspectingly eastward along the other side of the loch. And then, where the loch ends, he sprang out of the cool shade into the blazing July sun and set about Lovat and his shocked associates.

The Battle of Blar-na-Leine was an archetypal test to destruction. No quarter was expected or given. In such circumstances men, knowing the terms, will fight longer and with more ferocity than any animal. When their quivers were empty and their sweat-soaked garments discarded they butchered each other vigorously until the shadows lengthened, the shouts subsided and only gorging flies and a few – a very few – tottering men remained. No more than five Frasers and a handful of clansmen from Urquhart and Moriston left that bloody field, and they were burdened with the bodies of Lovat and Ranald Gallda, bound for burial in Beauly

Priory. Blar-na-Leine is commonly believed to mean the Field of the Shirts, because the clansmen stripped to their kilts in the summer heat: but in Gaelic it is Blar na Leana, the Field of the Swampy Meadow.

Revenge is said to be sweet. It occupied John of Moidart's mind as he planned punitive expeditions into the homelands of his enemies. Ewen Cameron – the first-born of Agnes Grant and Donald Cameron – with Alasdair of Glengarry and his son were to be their leaders. Ewen, of course, was Seumas' nephew. The Red Bard's treaty with the Camerons for mutual aid and support had become a bitter irony. The first raid was on lower Glenmoriston in 1544 and it resulted in much booty. The next year it was Glenurquhart's turn: an incursion so violent and prolonged that it left the land empty of cattle, the castle stripped to its boards and many houses burnt to the ground. It was impossible to seek military aid from the Crown – the Regent, Arran, was indolent and disinterested in clan feuding – so Seumas Grant and Iain Mor of Glenmoriston had to be content with legal action against the offenders. At the hearing in Inverness on 22nd October 1546 the defenders were absent as the cost of the damage and loss they had caused the two parishes was read out. This was quite enormous. Apart from the capital value of the livestock, of household goods and furniture, of stock feed, of boats and even of artillery stolen from the Castle, lost 'profits' were assessed at over £11,000, a tidy figure in those days even though the Scots pound had only a quarter the value of its English equivalent.

When the defenders remained silent much of their West Coast property and land was assigned by royal charter to Seumas Grant and Iain Mor, but possession was never physically achieved. But all this had put Lochiel in a less autocratic frame of mind and in 1548 he met his two uncles, Iain Mor and Seumas, to sign a non-aggression pact. Blood had cooled but bygones were not quite bygones for Seumas spent the rest of his life unsuccessfully trying to get some rents from his recently acquired West Coast lands.

Seumas Grant died in 1553 and his son John succeeded to the estate of Urquhart. These were lawless days in the Loch Ness basin and the new Laird of Grant was continually troubled by thieves and ruffians. The Queen Regent, Mary of Guise, allowed him to take the law into his own hands by appointing him a Justice over his estates on Loch Ness and Strathspey.

Ewen Cameron died in 1554, but the Camerons still coveted the rich pickings of livestock from Urquhart and Moriston. Rumours of an intended raid by them and the men of Clan Ranald reached the ears of Laird John. He sensibly asked the Crown for protection and in 1567 King James VI instructed the chiefs of Mackintosh and Kintail to combine in his defence. In the face of this powerful deterrent the would-be insurgents abandoned their plan and a grateful Laird of Grant married off his daughter to the Chief of Kintail.

The fierce clansmen civilised and romanticised by the Victorians. John Grant and John Fraser painted in the 1860s by Kenneth MacLeay for Queen Victoria. John Grant holds a Lochaber axe. The hook on the end was for pulling a mounted enemy off his horse.

The Queen of Scots was well thought of on Loch Ness-side and after her defeat at Langside and subsequent flight to England the local clans still supported her to a man. What can only be described as a protest march (and an occasionally rowdy one at that) was undertaken by the Grants of Urquhart and Moriston with powerful tenants, and their followers. They roamed the country from Inverness to beyond Aberdeen with banners and slogans, loudly acclaiming Mary's right to rule, but their case was hopeless as was hers and in the summer of 1569 the march ended. No action was taken against them.

Over in Glenmoriston Patrick, son of Iain Mor, died in 1581. His son John, who inherited the estates, was a colourful character. Like his grandfather he was big and powerful and to him the same name was given, Iain Mor, or Big John. As a man his judgement was respected and he was often asked to arbitrate in disputes, and so highly did the Laird of Grant think of his kinsman that he appointed him baron-bailie of Urquhart. Unfortunately this firm and effective man had a brutal, sadistic streak in him.

Legend has it that Big John, on a visit to Edinburgh, accepted the challenge of a loud-mouthed English wrestler whose reputation had deterred all other comers. At the start of the bout the two men shook hands, but Big John tightened his grip and broke all his opponent's fingers in a savage squeeze. Tales told round the peat fire tend to grow with the telling but the account of the killing of a tinker by Big John and two accomplices is documented fact. Macabre and brutal as it is, this murder seems to have had no motive. The three men waylaid the tinker in Glenmoriston, tied his hands, hanged him from a branch and then, having cut him down, mutilated his body with their dirks before burying him in a shallow grave in the bank of a stream. The murdered man's brother went to law but it was twenty years before the case was called in Edinburgh, and then Big John failed to appear. Surety paid into the court by Big John's kinsman, Grant of Carron, was forfeited, and the matter was dropped.

In 1603 the Loch-side's highest hill, Mealfuarvonie, was the scene of a bloody encounter, reminiscent in its fury of the battle of Blar-na-Leine. A year earlier the Mackenzies had taken the Macdonald's castle on the west coast at Strome, Loch Carron, and young Allan Dubh, son of Mac Ranald of Lundie, decided to teach them a lesson. Disguised as a tinker he spied out the land before leading his Glengarry followers to Muir of Ord on a Sunday morning in September. Then, so legend has it, he found the church of Kilchrist filled with worshipping Mackenzies, and promptly set fire to it. The terrified parishioners were impaled on the swords and dirks of the clansmen as they tried to escape while the Glengarry piper composed and played a pibroch as he marched round the burning building. Since that moment 'Kilchrist' has been the rallying song of the Clan.

Allan went on to vandalise the minister's library before stealing as many horses and cattle as his men could drive. The way home lay through part of Glenurquhart and over the moor from which Mealfuarvonie rises, and here they rested. But as news of the atrocity at Kilchrist spread Mackenzies dropped whatever they were doing, grabbed weapons and joined in the hunt.

A large force girdled the dome of Mealfuarvonie and fell upon the tired Glengarry men. They fought defensively but the Mackenzie volunteers were aflame with revenge. With them it was extermination or nothing and they almost achieved it; of his dead or dying company only Allan Dubh was fit enough to flee. At the western edge of the moor – henceforth known as the Lon na Fola, the Field of Blood – he found himself on a cliff top with a river gorge below; and on his heels were Mackenzies, yelling for his life. Without a backward glance he leapt across the chasm. The closest Mackenzie was less agile. He fell short and clutched at a sapling which Allan severed adroitly with his sword. 'I have left much with your race today, let me leave them that also' he remarked drily, as his victim, still clutching the stick, tumbled out of sight.

They say that the Devil looks after his own, and it is true that Allan Dubh avoided retribution. After further adventures he went to ground in a hill in Glengarry country, where he met a stonemason who fashioned him a tidy cave. For his services the kindly artisan lost his head; the distrustful Allan chopped it off in order to ensure secrecy as soon as the job was finished. His stay is remembered by the name Carn Mhic Raonuill, Macranald's Cairn, a hill north of Loch Lundie.

We seem to have wandered from Loch Ness but Allan Dubh's later life was influenced by the Lairds of Grant, whose vassal he was. This gave him a measure of protection, but in 1622 after a complaint had been brought against him by the Minister of Kilchrist 'his property and possessions were forfeited, and he himself declared an outlaw'. The Laird of Grant came to his vassal's rescue by buying the forfeited estates and allowing Allan grace-and-favour possession. In return Allan gave his solemn vow that he and his successors would be loyal to the Laird and his family for ever. This was of great advantage to both parties.

The MacGregors of that time seem to have been a troublesome lot and after a particularly brutal attack on Colquhoun of Luss the King was driven to proscribe them, and have them hunted down and killed, like mad dogs. Eventually the MacGregors were scattered far and wide. Since they shared a traditional clan origin with the Grants many made their way to Loch Ness-side. To harbour these outlaws was a grave offence and the lairds of Grant and Glenmoriston were heavily fined for such transgression. Under the law the lairds were responsible for clansmen's and tenants' acts and the full amount of the general fine – well over £10,000 in Scots money – fell to Grant to pay. The ungrateful MacGregor visitors did not mend their ways; in fact they proved a bad example to local men, encouraging all manner of delinquency among them.

Still the times were troubled – when were they not? – and in 1623 the Laird of Grant resolved to get a neglected Castle Urquhart back into defensive shape. A master mason named James Moray carried out the work, which included improvements to the headwall of the dungeon tower; he died in 1636 and his tombstone was found in the Drumnadrochit churchyard of Kilmore. Freshly mortared, the Castle waited for the next turn of events.

The principles of the Solemn League and Covenant, signed in 1643 by the House of Commons in return for Scottish support in the English Civil War, were regarded as unconstitutional by the Marquis of Montrose and others, and thus they gave their support to King Charles. In the north Alasdair MacColla, otherwise Lt.-Gen Sir Alexander Macdonald, cut a bloody swathe through the Great Glen as he marched at the head of Irish Troops to a camp near Fort Augustus. His draconian methods of warfare and Montrose's autocratic single-mindedness lost them many adherents. Only Glengarry and Clan Ranald supported them locally, attracting Macdonald clansmen from Urquhart and Glenmoriston. The Laird of Grant and his kinsman from across the hills sat back, like two owls, silent and indecisive. It is told that MacColla, while at Fort Augustus, commandeered a herd of cattle from Glenmoriston. The Laird's guardian (young John Grant was under-aged) wishing to favour neither side, gave orders that wild beasts from the highest ground should be rounded up. As they approached the camp the undomesticated cattle turned and madly rushed back to the wilderness, just as the guardian had planned.

MacColla was joined by Montrose at Blair Atholl, and there followed that series of victories over the Covenanters that eventually ended in a bloodbath in the shadow of Ben Nevis when 1500 Campbells were killed. Many were impressed by such successful shows of strength and the Laird of Grant was one of them. He sent Montrose 300 men, a gesture for which he soon paid when Covenanters at Inverness plundered his house there. His mother, the Lady of Urquhart (who had always been a vociferous royalist), suffered even more. She was robbed of all her possessions and driven from the Castle in the Christmas of 1644. Although, once again, the stronghold was stripped to its bare boards, there is no record of structural damage. The parish lost many of its men at the Battle of Auldearn.

Montrose was defeated at Philliphaugh in 1645, but returned to the North in an attempt to take Inverness from the Covenanters. General Middleton came to its relief and drove the marquis back through Glenmoriston, Fort Augustus and Stratherrick into Strathspey. Montrose was by no means beaten; in Glenmoriston he had given the Covenanters a bloody time of it. But then the King, held by the Scottish army in England, told him to disperse his army and seek safety for himself on the Continent.

The Laird of Grant enthusiastically supported Charles II in his attempt to retake the Stuart throne. After his landing in 1650 the Laird sent him 1400 men under the

ntrose

57

command of his brother, Grant of Clunemore. A year later the Scots were decisively beaten at Worcester and only a few of the men of Urquhart returned to their homes. Cromwell marched triumphantly into Scotland, and established a garrison at Inverness. Despite his powerful military presence there was still some support for the King in far-flung glens, and another battle had to be fought and lost before it became clear that Cromwell's grip on the Highlands was a firm one. Both the Laird of Grant and Macdonald of Glengarry gave the Lord Protector assurances of their good will and behaviour on payment of a bond which in Glengarry's case amounted to £2000 in Scots money.

Cromwell, despite his many faults, was a prudent and practical man. As part of his policing policy he caused a forty-ton ship, armed with four cannon, to be built in Inverness and manhandled, using ropes and rollers, to Lochend. A contemporary account by a Commonwealth trooper gives a light-hearted description of how this was accomplished. He tells in some detail why 'an English ship, by curious invention, was haled over the mountains to this solitary Lough; brought hither on purpose to reclaim the Highlander.'

Whether or not the Highlander was reclaimed the ensuing decade under the firm rule of the Commonwealth was a period of peace and security. Writing at this time the Minister of Wardlaw, a man of royalist sympathies, applauded the cheapness and quality of commodities which the English had brought to Inverness. 'They not only civilised but enriched this place' he says, and goes on to speak, like the trooper, of 'the statly friggot' without a hint of rancour at its policing function.

For eight years a strict but even-handed administration suppressed internecine clan strife and curbed local civil disobedience. Then Cromwell died and two years later the Stuart dynasty was restored. It was far from being an unmixed blessing; it was the signal for a resumption of the bad, old ways on Loch Ness-side, and elsewhere. The Laird of Grant was commissioned to form a group with the authority to make citizens' arrests, and he supplied labour for the task of demolishing the Citadel in Inverness in 1662. The King saw this act as a gesture to his loyal chiefs; to the disaffected it was rather a sign that the law was becoming lax. Vendettas were common, worked out with acts of arson. Four years later the Castle was repaired again; as the cost of the work was less than £150 (Scots) it couldn't have amounted to much.

In 1688 William of Orange took the throne from James II and VII. The Highland army which supported the deposed king was led by John Graham of Claverhouse. General Hugh Mackay, who had done good service for William on the Continent, opposed him. Sir Ludovick Grant of Strathspey and Urquhart, who had succeeded his father James, was Mackay's man; his kinsmen John Grant of Glenmoriston, with Grant of Shewglie (in Glenurquhart) and Glengarry took Graham's side. The inevitable battle was at a place called Rinrory, and the Highlanders won but

Drawn by David Allan   from the original at Keith Castle

Viscount Dundee

*Dark blue Eyes, Eybrows & hair colour
= between black & Brown*

John Graham
of Claverhouse,
'Bonnie
Dundee'

Claverhouse was killed.

We are now reaching the end of Castle Urquhart's active life. It was to close with both a bang and a whimper. The garrison which had strongly held it for two years after the collapse of the rebellion on the death of Claverhouse, blew up part of it on leaving in order to render it useless to the Jacobites. Huge sections of masonry preserved to this day bear witness to powerful explosives. Soon the shattered building, whose long and varied fortunes had been those of the Loch-side on which it stands, was the victim of vandalism, tons of lead being stripped from its roof, and timbers from inside. In February 1715 a great storm of wind toppled the south west walls which collapsed down a cliff whose steepness is matched below water level.

An 18th-century view of Castle Urquhart

4 Wade, Charles Edward, Boswell and Johnson

THINGS WERE not going well in the Highlands in the 18th century. The unsuccessful Jacobite risings of 1715 and 1719 were damp squibs, lit almost at random. The first ended, in our area of the Great Glen, when Glengarry and Keppoch surrendered to General Cadogan at Inverness; Cadogan had shown a touch of gunboat diplomacy in sailing his naval pinnace through Loch Ness to Loch Oich. The 1719 affair was also smartly terminated at Glen Shiel, not far from Loch Ness; on 10th June of that year Lovat and Clanranald, with some clansmen and five hundred Spanish regulars, were seen off by the Government forces under General Wightman who had marched from the strong garrison at Inverness. It was a diversionary affair, unsupported by events further south, and it was reckoned at the time that the Jacobites and their Spanish companions 'seemed not very fond of the enterprise'.

The Disarming Act that followed the 1715 rising was bitterly resented by loyal clans. While they had scrupulously handed in their arms, the disaffected kept their own weapons hidden and submitted worn out and sub-standard pieces which had been imported for the deception; the inevitable result of this was that in contemporary disputes between them the honest, unarmed clans were at a fatal disadvantage. This state of affairs was made much of, for his own ends, by the wily Simon Fraser, Lord Lovat. His seat was at Dounie Castle, some six miles as the crow flies from Loch Ness. In a memorandum to King George in 1724 Lovat

Simon Fraser, Lord Lovat, portrayed by Hogarth shortly before his execution as a traitor in 1746.

painted, with self-seeking relish, the blackest possible picture of his countrymen, accusing them of backwardness, barbarity and anarchy. He spoke of the widespread practice of what today would be called 'protection'. He referred to the Highland Companies, formed after the 1689 rising in King William's reign, as a highly effective means of keeping the law which, in fact, they were not. He warmly advocated their reform under his personal control. Being the highly devious man he was, there seems little doubt that he saw the chance of organising crime on the grand scale. King George, knowing something of him, was not at all convinced that this was a good idea. He wanted a second opinion and there was no better person to give it than one of his most trusted generals, George Wade.

Wade was the grandson of a certain Major William Wade who had received lands in Ireland in lieu of pay from Oliver Cromwell. In this respect his family history was not unlike that of Lord Cadogan; his grandfather, too, had been set up by the Lord Protector. From the day of his birth George was intended for the Army (of his two brothers the eldest inherited the Wade estates and the other went into the Church as was often the custom) and in 1690, at the age of seventeen, he was gazetted ensign in the 10th Foot. A brave and resourceful soldier, his promotion was steady. He twice commanded troops in Flanders and distinguished himself at the siege of Liége. By 1703 he had become Lieutenant-Colonel. As second-in-command of a force sent to destroy the garrison of Fort St. Minorca he had his first taste of military road construction on what was then a roadless island. With the coming of peace in 1711 he went on the retired list at the age of 38 and was shortly afterwards returned to Parliament for Hindon in Wiltshire.

By 1715 he was back on active service but now he combined military command with the functions of an intelligence officer. The city of Bath was rife with plots aimed at restoring the Stuart dynasty, of which Wade was an industrious foiler. His discovery of a huge cache of arms was overshadowed by his penetration of a conspiracy to depose George I. Evidence pointed to the Swedish Ambassador as being implicated and Wade, dispensing with diplomatic courtesies, cordoned off his London house. He arrested the Ambassador, Count Gyllenborg, as he was in the act of destroying official papers and a search revealed a wealth of incriminating evidence. King George was greatly satisfied with Wade and made him colonel of the 3rd Dragoon Guards. Then he was off to Spain where he further distinguished himself. For two years, from 1722, there was another intermission in his military career; he was once again the politician, being elected Member of Parliament for Bath. His popularity there ensured a safe seat which he held until his death in 1748, although during these years he was often an absentee member.

With such a record of loyal and efficient service it is not, then, surprising that King George saw Wade as just the man to sort out the troublesome Highlanders. To this end the general was ordered to assess the whole situation and to suggest 'such remedies as may conduce to the quiet of his Majesty's faithful subjects, and the good settlement of that part of the Kingdom'. Wade set out for the Highlands on the 4th July 1724, and reported to the King in December. His findings, though much more impartial than Lovat's, revealed a state of affairs much as the other described. Lovat's personal policing, however, was not one of Wade's remedies.

He did propose the revival of the Highland Companies, but under incorruptible management; he pointed out the ways in which the former companies, raised by King William, had failed by not 'being put under proper Regulations' and how bribery had often allowed criminals to go free. He proposed the building of a Fort at Inverness (later known as Fort George) and a better situated one at Killihuimen (later Fort Augustus); he wanted a boat with sails and oars, big enough to carry up to eighty soldiers, to ensure adequate communications and the swift movement of troops along Loch Ness; he called for honest men to administer the law and the establishment of Quarter Sessions at Killihuimen, Ruthven (in the Spey valley), Fort William and, if the situation called for it, at Bernera (Glenelg). Finally he demanded effective punishment for carrying and concealing arms: a fine was seldom paid because of the transgressor's poverty, and Wade believed that parliament should not shrink from imposing harsher penalties.

This report appears to have been well received, for Wade was at once appointed Commander of the Forces in North Britain with full authority to build his boat, the new forts at Killihuimen and Inverness, and for that endeavour for which he is most commonly remembered, 'the mending of the Roads between Garrisons and Barracks, for the better Communication of his Majesty's Troops'. He hoped that it could be done within two years at a cost 'not exceeding £10,000 per annum'. That it took rather longer and cost more is the common experience of those before and after Wade who have had the spleen to tackle great works in the awkward Highlands, with their weather, bogs, rocks, rivers and independent people.

Wade came to Scotland in 1725 and at once began to build his first Inverness to Fort Augustus road. This, on the south-east side, only touched the Loch at its western end. It took the present line which rises steeply from Inverness over Drumashie Moor and squeezes between the dungeon-like cliffs of Tom Bailgeann and the narrow Loch Ceo-Ghlas before crossing the River Farigaig at Torness. Thereafter it becomes fugitive, a mere shadow in the heather, as it merges with, or parts from, the modern road on its way to Fort Augustus.

Wade, who favoured the shortest way between garrisons, was not content with this circuitous route. By the summer of 1732 he had laid another road almost at water level through to Foyers. Boswell and Johnson used this way, forty years later, pausing at the 'Druid Temple' a few miles out of Inverness (see p. 29). Though certainly more direct, it called for courageous engineering. The General stated casually, in a letter to George II, that above 2000 yards of it was cut through solid rock. The working of this section, just east of Inverfarigaig, was a laborious business. The conglomerate precipice that dropped sheer into the water had to be blasted away with gunpowder; the miners hung by ropes as they hammered the charge holes into the pebbly face. It must have been the very devil to drill, each stone in the matrix deflecting the tool, and since the rock is seamless the explosives would have produced a spatter of material rather than a general collapse. It is immense credit to Wade, as engineer-contractor, that he imbued his officers and men with a spirit of competition. He also put them all on double pay.

No sooner was the Black Rock, as it is called, behind them than they were presented with a different problem. Half a mile to the west the River Farigaig tumbles to Loch Ness through a steep-sided ravine. The bridge Wade constructed (at the cost of £150) was a solid achievement, still used well into the first half of the present century. But at Foyers even the indomitable General had to leave the Loch for the hilly country to the south-east, and from that village to Fort Augustus both the 1726 and 1732 roads followed the same course and are now overlaid by the modern B 862. The exact site of Wade's working office, long known as the General's Hut, cannot be precisely located, but it must have been quite close to the Foyers Hotel.

Wade was a man of many parts. As an engineer his work is lasting and self-evident. In the Great Glen roads and bridges were only some of it. His grand strategic design demanded strong, well sited forts, so arranged as to intercept the lines of rebel communication and movement. In support of this object he added a barracks with an outer wall on Inverness Castle Hill where there had been some sort of fort ever since the 12th century. This new building, called Fort George, was blown up by the Jacobites in 1746. It was burnt out and not restored, but its name was transferred to the big barracks at Ardersier, begun two years later in 1748. At Fort Augustus the General was dissatisfied with the position of the 1716 fort which stood in what is the middle of the present village, south of the canal. His plan was for a building large enough to house 300 men, and strong enough to mount twelve guns. Work on it was started in 1727 and lasted for fifteen years. It, like Inverness, was severely damaged by the Jacobites, who blew up the powder magazine. St Benedict's Abbey now occupies its site which, as Wade intended, is only a stone's throw from the Loch. Finally, following Cromwell's example, Wade soon had his galley sailing on Loch Ness. On her first trip she caused a local stir, with her gay flags and the sound of her eight guns fired in practice. A harbour was made for her in the mouth of the River Tarff, and she must have been well maintained for in the early 19th century she was taking soundings for the Caledonian Canal.

There is little doubt that George Wade's influence was for the good of the Highlands. As under Cromwell, order was maintained in the Glens; men and women could sleep easy in their beds. Wade gave prudent counsel to George I and II to counterbalance that from the disaffected, and as a ruler over an oppressed majority

Loch Ness

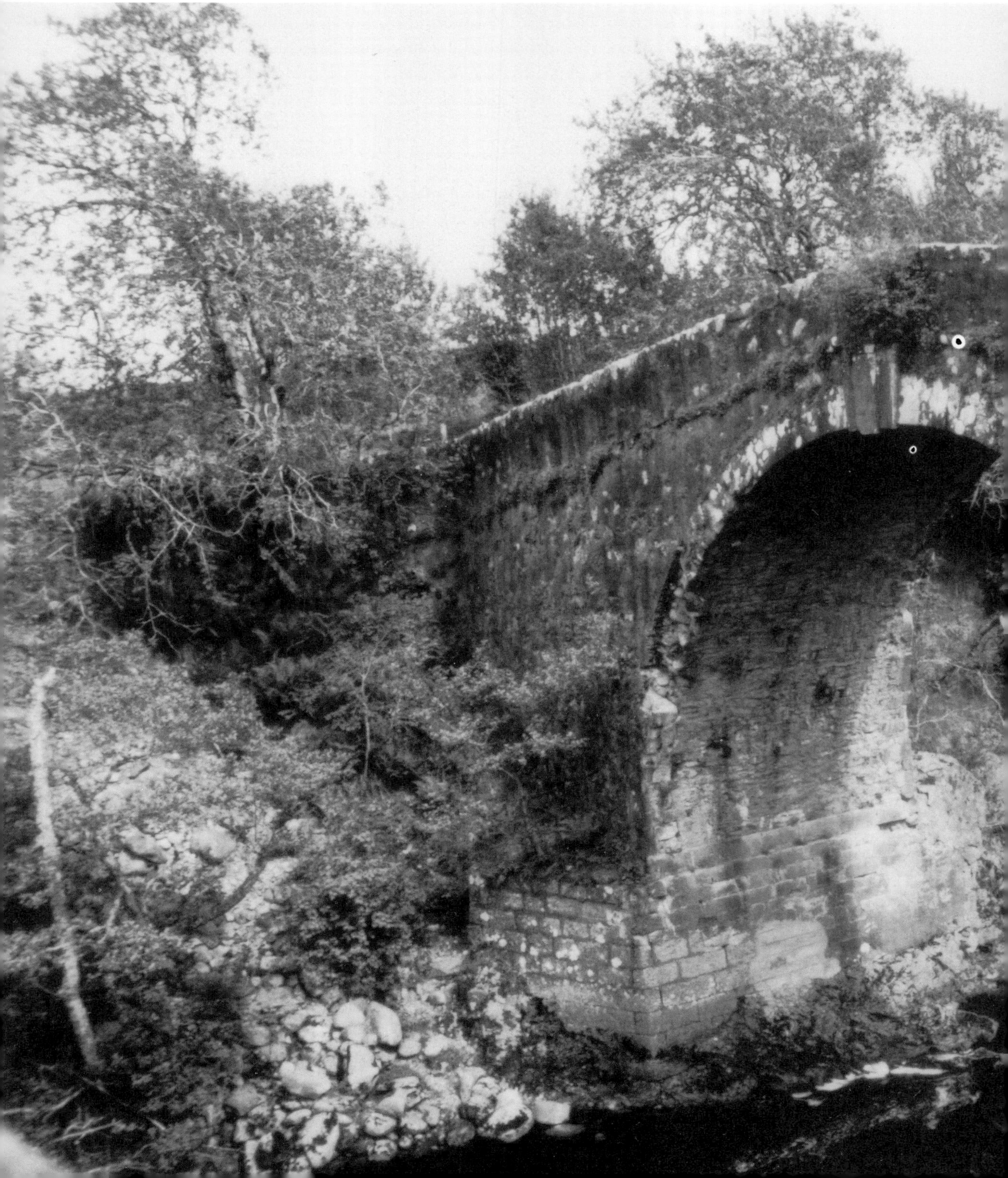

*General
Wade's Bridge
over the River
Farigaig*

he was stern but just. Yet he is remembered less for his sound administration and exercise of humanity than for his civil engineering. Ironically his roads brought much benefit to the Stuart cause. There was not a mile of them that was not put to use by Charles Edward's armies in advance or retreat.

In July 1745 Charles Edward, that most improvident of princes, landed, with seven friends, at Loch nan Uamh in Morar. In all honesty it was a black moment for Scotland. Two years earlier France had been all ready to invade England with 15,000 men, the prince among them, but a storm broke up the armada, interest in the project evaporated and thereafter there was nothing but hollow promises from that country and from Spain. Charles, the blind visionary and airy optimist, decided to go ahead, land and hope then to rally support. An Opinion Poll, taken at that moment, would have shown a huge number of 'don't knows' and could have brought little comfort to the Jacobites. From its inception this disastrous rising – in which as usual, the common people, many of whom were innocent bystanders, bore the main brunt of the killing and misery – pitted romantic adherence to a lost cause against good plain common sense and prudence. Most governments were oppressive and the Hanoverians, if left unprovoked, were no worse than any other.

The Castle 1728–1746

Inverness Castle, the first Fort George

Charles, having let it be known in the right quarters that he had landed, raised his provocative standard at Glenfinnan and marched, with some growing support, to Fort Augustus at the end of August. Then, taking General Wade's new road over Corrieyairack and its continuation through the Drumochter pass, he was in Perth by the 4th September. Meantime, at Castle Grant in Speyside, Ludovick Grant, direct descendant of the Red Bard, cautioned his tenants in the barony of Urquhart to stay quietly in their homes or risk his extreme displeasure. On the other hand the heads of three powerful Glenurquhart families and Patrick Grant of Glenmoriston (who was connected to Ludovick in ancient blood) declared for the prince, and a representative contingent of some 350 men followed in Charles's foot-steps towards Edinburgh. They were just in time to throw their weight into the defeat of the inept Sir John Cope at Prestonpans and, indeed, many of them were still with the Jacobite army on the bloody field of Culloden.

The rout at Prestonpans and subsequent successes produced a state of euphoria in the prince's supporters. The time had come to hammer home the message. A young colonel was sent on a propaganda visit to Urquhart with the news that he was 'clad with the Prince's orders to burn and harass all people that does not immediately joyn the standard'. In the event he settled for impassioned exhortation and fair promises. Ludovick Grant, anxious to display his neutrality, demanded that his tenants should be transferred to Speyside out of the reach of such sedition, and his Urquhart factor managed to round up sixty or so bemused men. At Upper Drumbuie, on the old road to Inverness, they were stopped by the colonel and powerful local Jacobites who swore that if the tenants did not at once return, their crops and cattle would suffer. Hardly knowing what to think the miserable men went home.

The centre of activity shifted further and further from the Highlands until the prince's advance petered out at Derby. But by the 18th February 1746 he was in Inverness where he was joined by sixty Urquhart men. Fort George, commanded by Ludovick Grant's uncle, surrendered smartly, and was mined and destroyed. The Jacobite forces went on to take Fort Augustus, bombarding Wade's new fort with mortars fired from the ramparts of the old. Fort William, however, was a nut they failed to crack, and it was a significant failure.

In Aberdeen the 25-year-old Cumberland was biding his time. With fresh and disciplined troops he began to move towards Inverness on the 8th April. It was six days before news of this reached the Jacobites and urgent calls were sent out to men who had temporarily returned to their homes. Among these were men of Loch Ness-side. By the time they reached Inverness it was also time to fight. The Battle of Culloden between the Jacobites and the government troops was short and brutish. Cumberland, sadistic and thorough, managed his part of it with Teutonic effici-ency. On both sides the soldiers fought with that cold desperation which came from knowing that no quarter or mercy was expected or given. Charles over-ruled the advice of experienced officers and paid the price, though that same price would have had to be paid, sooner or later.

Impetuous, stubborn, essentially impractical yet possessed of a dangerous charm, Charles had sown the wind; it was the men and women of the north who reaped the whirlwind. It blew first on Urquhart, already robbed of thirty of its men by the battle or by its deplorable aftermath. Ludovick Grant gave up his seat on the fence and showed his high respect for Government by organising witch hunts against the defeated rebels. With a large force he scoured the area but the hiding places were unknown to Speyside men and his haul was small. In order to increase it, he made it known that the Jacobites of Urquhart and Glenmoriston should seek royal clemency, inferring, at the least, that such action would result in a degree of amnesty. Some men were rightly dubious and did not show their faces, but eighty-four of their companions, from both glens, came complete with arms to an arranged gathering place at Balmacaan in Glenurquhart. They were taken to Cumberland in Inverness, and thence to London. With three exceptions the victims of Grant's duplicity were transported to Barbados. Government was less than grateful to Ludovick. He was denied the expenses incurred in his search for rebels, and in July his estate of Urquhart was ravaged by a company of English soldiers. Inevitably his remaining tenants were the main sufferers.

The whirlwind blew long and strong in Glenmoriston. Invermoriston House was wilfully burnt to the ground by a group of Macleods and Macdonalds from Skye who subsequently ran amok in the glen, destroying all they could find. It was dark, perverse behaviour in men who had been in two minds whether to join the Stuart cause, but the people's tribulation really began when, on the 24th May, Cumberland made his headquarters in Fort Augustus. Numerous tales exist of unprovoked murder, rape, theft and arson, all carried out with the apparent approval of the supreme commander. With their homes destroyed and their cattle carried away, many died of hunger and exposure in the bleak winter of 1746. Within the Fort it was a different story. The sale of plundered livestock provided prize-money for the NCOs and privates who created a black market in saleable commodities. The men ate well, and horse racing was introduced as a necessary recreation. Under threat of dire punishment not a crust of bread might be given or sold to the starving glens-people; the conquerers were neither generous nor even just to the defeated High-landers.

While all this was going on, the young man whose ill-judged disturbance of the political status quo had brought it about, was still on the run. With a £30,000 reward on his head he crossed to the West after Culloden and reached the Outer Hebrides. Hotly pursued (and greatly helped by Miss Macdonald's ingenious decep-tion) he got to Morar, on the mainland once more, on the 5th July. Here the net

Wade, Charles Edward, Boswell and Johnson

The Duke of Cumberland, son of George II
and victor at Culloden

The *BATTLE* of CULLODEN, near Inverneſs in *SCOTLAND*, 16ᵗʰ April 1746.

The Kings Army Commanded by the Duke of Cumberland was drawn up in three Lines, into the left of which the Rebels attempting to break with
Swords and Targets were repulsed: when Kingston's Horse attack'd the left Wing, and the Dragoons the Rear; which compleated the Rout of the
Rebels, who had 2500 Men kill'd in the Battle, 1500 in the Pursuit and 1800 taken Prisoners.
Printed for & Sold by CARINGTON BOWLES, at his Map & Print Warehouse, Nº69 in Sᵗ Pauls Church Yard, LONDON.

SIR LUDOVICK GRANT OF GRANT, BARONET.
B 13TH JANUARY 1707. D. 18TH MARCH 1773.

The second Fort George, begun in 1748 on the coast to the east of Inverness.

began to close and he was indeed fortunate to find three resourceful companions, and later a local man who knew the area, to help him through the difficult days that followed. From Glenshiel they crossed the watershed between east and west at Cluanie where, alarmed by the sound of shots, they took to the mountains.

Perhaps these same shots killed Roderick Mackenzie; the exact date of his death is not known but it was after Charles's return from the Hebrides, and the location is correct. Mackenzie, who was a devoted Jacobite and member of the Prince's bodyguard, was footloose in the Highlands, following Culloden. Near Ceannacroc, some twelve miles from Loch Ness, at the mouth of the Coire Dho, he was surprised by a party of redcoats. Mackenzie bore a strong resemblance to his leader which the soldiers, very conscious of a £30,000 reward, were quick to mark. They made every effort to take Mackenzie alive but he resisted so violently that they were forced to shoot him. His last words, 'You have killed your Prince', led to the removal of his head for identification elsewhere, and a slackening of the search for the real Prince who may, quite possibly, have been close by.

At any rate Charles and his companions entered the Coire Dho and climbed to near its top where they spent a vastly uncomfortable night in a rocky crevice at well

73

over 2000 feet. The Prince had heard earlier that French ships were at Poolewe (in Wester Ross) and wanted to get there if he could. The local man did not know the route to the coast but, by a happy chance, there were others hiding in this same corrie who did. The Seven Men of Glenmoriston were partisans who had sworn together never to surrender or to cease harrying Government troops and informers. They sprang at the chance to help the Prince to safety, welcomed him to their cave, took a further oath of fidelity to his person and entertained him, as royally as the situation allowed, for three days. Their loyalty is recorded on a plaque at the entrance. Later, for safety's sake, they removed to another cave nearby and finally left the Coire Dho on the 6th August. During that month there were many forced marches, twists and turns, comings and goings and near brushes with the pursuers, but eventually the Glenmoriston men brought Charles into contact with the wounded Lochiel, and relative security. The Prince and the Cameron chief escaped to France in September.

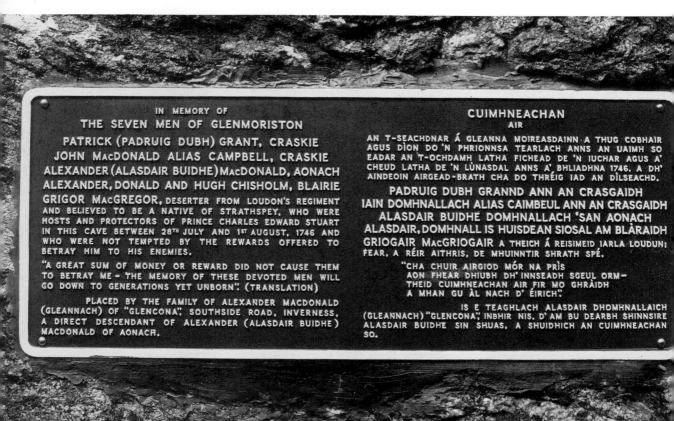

And that, if we overlook a few executions at Tyburn (including Simon Fraser, Lord Lovat) and a host of repressive measures, was that. The rash Jacobite dream, which had turned to nightmare, was ended. Some romantic novelists, and other storytellers, represent these Jacobite risings as popular expressions of universal discontent. This they plainly were not, being, rather, blatant examples of coercion and propaganda; and it is arguable whether the lives of the oppressed and much afflicted common people would have been any better under Stuart rule.

On Monday 30th August 1773 Dr. Samuel Johnson and his friend James Boswell set out from Inverness to ride to Fort Augustus. They did not get under way until 9 a.m. as one of the horses needed a shoe and the smith was unwell after a wedding. They might have taken their post-chaise as far as Fort Augustus but decided against it as they could get no horses west of Inverness. In the event they were happy to ride on a bright early Autumn morning.

Cumberland's camp outside Fort Augustus, by his secretary Thomas Sandby, July 1746

Soon they reached a Druid Temple. In his account of the trip the doctor makes no mention of it, but Boswell reports that his comment was dismissive and derogatory; his friend had no great care for ancient things. It is a view still prevalent. After searching for this neolithic place the other day I came across it almost by chance; it is quite hidden by bramble, gorse, scrub and bracken. These stones have

View from the mouth of the cave where Prince Charles hid with the Seven Men of Glenmoriston

stood as long as the Egyptian pyramids, and their age, if nothing else, has earned them respect (see p. 29).

Johnson approved of Wade's road, remarking that the surface was so hard and level that the horses needed no guiding. It allowed the travellers to look about them. Across the loch the doctor saw rocks 'towering in horrid nakedness' (certainly the shattered face of the Abriachan granite) but neither he nor his companion were cast into depression by it. Twenty-seven years earlier a volunteer in Cumberland's army, quartered at Fort Augustus, had remarked that the sight 'of the black barren mountains covered with snow and streams of water rolling down them was sufficient to give a well-bred dog the vapours, and occasioned numbers to fall sick daily as well in their minds as their bodies.' It is interesting to reflect on how attitudes to wild terrain have changed – nowadays tourists will pay money to admire such sights – although Johnson's view of the Loch in 1773 today incorporates the hideous scar made by the builders of the road on the north-east side.

He was pretty well-informed about the dimensions of the Loch – twenty-four miles long by one to two miles broad – and as to its depth, surprisingly so. Though he seems to have accepted that it was filled partly by springs in its bed and that its water was considered medicinal (at which the shade of Daly the Druid must have nodded smugly), he cast doubts on the claim that it was, in places, 840 feet deep, a figure only established within the last two decades. He mused on another claim, that ice never formed on its surface, and in doing so remarked, 'That which is strange is delightful, and a pleasing error is not willingly detected' – a statement from high literary authority which gives an ebullient writer like myself reasonable carte blanche, as well as encapsulating the driving force behind the Loch Ness Monster industry. He concluded that 'Lough (sic) Ness well deserves to be diligently examined'. No one can deny that his advice has been followed thoroughly, even ad nauseam.

Boswell, too, appears to have been in a cheerful mood. Still untouched by the spoiling hands of 'progress' and commercial exploitation, the Loch behind its screen of delicate green birch, alder and hazel, dark blue water reflecting pale blue sky, inspired him to observe that 'the scene was as remote and agreeably wild as could be desired'. As they jogged along the military road, with Joseph Ritter, Boswell's servant, and two Highlanders on foot, Boswell thoughtfully studied his older friend against an unfamiliar background. Mr. Johnson, he wrote, rode very well.

After travelling some miles along the Loch they came to a rough dwelling, the first they had seen. Johnson's interests lay more with people than places, and they stopped and made an uninvited entry. The doctor invoked the 'old laws of hospitality' to justify this intrusion. The hut stood at the water's edge, presumably on a narrow grass strip between the steep banks and the Loch. It was built in the beehive

78

style with a raftered roof thatched with heath. It was a large example of its kind, and contained several apartments. The low walls were of loosely piled stones, and heating and cooking were provided by a fire whose acrid smoke escaped through a hole in the roof.

Inside they found a woman cooking goat's flesh. She had little or no English but one of the Highlanders interpreted for them. In Boswell's account we are told that the woman was afraid that the doctor wished to go to bed with her, and the incident was the source of some mild ribaldry between them later. Johnson, on the other hand, is silent upon it. He was plainly shocked at such a state of housing 'in one of the nations of this opulent and powerful island' and we feel that he was simply bursting to tell the innocents about their nakedness, like the well-meaning missionary who brings nothing but grief and good tidings. Through the woman's few words of English, and the help of the interpreter, the travellers learned that she was Mrs Fraser, and had five children, the eldest being thirteen years old. Her husband was a man of eighty, still apparently hale, whose landlord employed him as a forester, in return for which service he had the bothy and permission to keep sixty goats on the ground.

She went on to tell them that two of her sons were in Inverness, buying oatmeal which was expensive but could not be done without. Her sixty goats for milk and flesh, with some hens, potatoes and barley, supplied their needs. She told her questioners that she was as happy as any woman in Scotland, though any nuance of tone may have been lost in the translation. At any rate, 'Mr Johnson was pleased at seeing for the first time such a state of human life'.

Boswell & Johnson set out on their Highland jaunt from Edinburgh: a caricature by Rowlandson

The inquisition over, Mrs Fraser offered them all whisky in true Highland style. Though so much has changed on Loch Ness-side, that custom remains sacrosanct. Boswell, Joseph and the Highlanders took a dram, the doctor demurred. Mrs Fraser expressed a liking for snuff but her visitors had none; instead each of them offered her sixpence and a further sixpence, it would seem, for the whisky. This insult passed unremarked, and, with mutual expressions of good will, the travellers continued on their journey.

The next stop was the General's Hut, Wade's former site office, now used as an inn. Johnson said that it was not 'ill stocked with provisions' while Boswell describes the menu which included a bottle of Malaga. One is inclined to the belief that he must have drunk too much of that as he fails to mention their subsequent visit to the Loch's then best-known beauty spot, the Falls of Foyers. Johnson, however, speaks of it in detail, and tells how they 'clambered over very rugged crags' as they approached the lip of the waterfall from the bridge on the military road. At length they halted so close to the edge of the 'horrid chasm' that 'we were naturally inclined to turn away our heads'. Despite his unease he regretted that a dry spell – which pleased them in every other way – had strangled the full flow of the torrent, and he took time to imagine how it would be when 'a thousand streams' were added to the trickle. If he had returned in the spirit 123 years later his regret might have changed to wonder, for in 1896 the British Aluminium Company harnessed the proud River Foyers to industrial ends and commanded the water as they saw fit.

Given their nine a.m. start from Inverness and the halts on the journey, it must have been late afternoon before the party started along the weary road that separates Fort Augustus from Foyers. Joseph and one of the Highlanders were sent ahead to tell Governor Trapaud (a friend of Boswell's father, the judge) of their expected arrival and, in due course, they were well received. Boswell speaks of the Governor's house as being 'neat and well furnished, with prints etc.', standing in 'a well built little square' and they enjoyed a good supper which included fricassee of moor fowl. There was a civilised evening with their hosts and thereafter, I do not doubt, a long dreamless sleep.

In the morning they enjoyed the Governor's garden and inspected his fort. They took a look at the sloop. One of the officers, with whom they breakfasted, had been in America and spoke about the Indians. Johnson sympathised with their condition as much as with that of the defeated Highlanders; he was really a Jacobite sympathiser, and ever a supporter of the underdog.

At mid-day they were on the move once more, mounting the zig-zags of the military road which would carry them over the hill into Invermoriston. From here they must have enjoyed a fine panoramic view of the Loch before it was hidden behind the swell of the moor. That night they arrived at the inn at Anoch. No trace remains of it today but from Boswell's estimate of 'eleven wild miles' it could not have been far from Ceannacroc Bridge where Roderick Mackenzie was killed, and not much further from the wild harbour of the Prince and his Glenmoriston men.

Their host was named Macqueen; in Boswell's words he 'was a sensible fellow' and he was proud of his learning. The travellers' overt surprise at his small library was taken as a condescension and not well received. In fact Macqueen was a scholar who read poetry in Latin and wrote it in Gaelic. It also transpired that he was 'a gentleman of the old Highland stamp – married to a laird's daughter', and he had been an active Jacobite, and with the Prince at Culloden. His reasons for keeping an inn included a wish to exhibit the common touch, an attitude which persists in Highland gentlemen-innkeepers to this day, though most would deny it. Though his fare was solid and his conversation good his building was very poor – being constructed of loose stones, thick turf and thatched with turf and twigs – and quite unlike Governor Trapaud's pleasant billet of the night before.

Boswell & Johnson dining at the new Fort George outside Inverness: a drawing by E Shepard

DINNER WITH THE 37TH AT FORT GEORGE

81

The travellers met Macqueen's daughter, an attractive well-spoken lass, who had been schooled in Inverness in the 'common female qualifications'. Johnson was quite taken by her confident manners and civil responses. He gave her a book, Cocker's *Arithmetic*, for, as he was to remark later, 'a book of science is inexhaustible'.

They spent an uncomfortable night at the Anoch Inn; Boswell feared infestation by vermin, both men had night-fears that Macqueen, who had stated his intention of emigrating because of the high cost of rents, might murder them for their money. It was an ungenerous thought. In the morning their host accompanied them some way towards the west. As they rode he told them moving tales about Culloden and Boswell was more than once reduced to tears. After Macqueen had turned back they crossed the watershed and dropped down into Glenshiel, leaving Loch Ness far behind.

Johnson in his 'Travelling Dress'

5 Telford's Canal and the Railway That Never Was

IN THE year of Johnson's Highland visit, 1773, James Watt, the developer of the steam engine, was asked to report on the viability of a ship canal between Fort William and Inverness. The Commissioners who adminstered the estates which had been forfeit to the Crown by reason of their owners' support of the Jacobite cause, saw such a project as a useful way of absorbing the Highlanders' rebellious energies. The county of Inverness was relatively overpopulated and rents were high; Fort William's first shipload of emigrants was already on the high seas, bound for America. There were all the ingredients for unrest.

Watt suggested that sections of canal, ten feet deep, could be used to link the three lochs of the Great Glen and join them to the seas, for £164,000. Nothing was done about his report. But in the late 18th century canals were all the rage and the idea was not long allowed to lapse. Local landowners saw profit in it, the British Fisheries Society (an organisation set up to promote the herring industry) were enthusiastic, and Government, enmeshed in its endless war with Fance, was aware of its military advantages and prepared to foot the bill. The Great Glen waterway was thus to become an early example of state-promoted civil engineering.

In 1801 Thomas Telford, the gifted son of a Dumfriesshire shepherd, was at the height of his fame as an engineer. With the Ellesmere Canal and other successful works to his credit he was the obvious man to pronounce upon the project's feasability. He talked it all over with his friend James Watt and then went north to carry out a survey. The Loch Ness Galley from Fort Augustus, which had once been used for gunboat diplomacy, was employed to take soundings at Lochend and the shallow Loch Oich. Telford, elated by the challenge, reported to his masters that the job could be completed in seven years for a mere £350,000. In the event it was to cost rather more and take much longer. Such delays have a familiar ring about them, but it was ironic that the war ended and there was still no useable waterway, even between Loch Ness and the Moray Firth.

To Telford, well versed in such things, it had not looked daunting; to an ignorant layman it seemed simplicity itself. The long, straight rift of the Great Glen, carved by God in his own time and two-thirds filled with water at no extra expense, appeared so apt for canalisation that the engineer had stated that he had 'observed no serious obstacle in any part of it'. One Inverness minister remarked airily that 'Nature has left little to be done'. A century earlier the Brahan Seer, a Highland Isaiah of some repute, had abandoned prophecy for a calculated guess when he spoke of the time, not far in the future, 'when full rigged ships will be seen sailing eastward and westward by the back of Tomnahurich at Inverness'. It reminds one of Tennyson's impassioned 1840s forecast of aerial warfare in 'Locksley Hall' when no aircraft had ever yet flown. But in the Great Glen Nature had, in fact, left quite a lot to be done. The ice which had rounded and deepened the fault had left a lot of debris on its floor in the form of sand and gravel and such material will not retain water. Also, of course, these deposits lay at varying depths in the valley so that the surface levels of these three vastly convenient lochs were different. Loch Ness' surface is fifty feet above the sea, a fact idiotically disregarded by those who speak of subterranean passages to the Atlantic; Loch Oich is higher at 106 feet; Loch Lochy slightly lower. This called for the provision of locks and gates, a need at once apparent to Telford though probably not to the Inverness minister!

To the stated problems were added a host of imponderables, but Telford never seems to have lost heart. He had a good team on the whole and a conviction that he was engaged in 'one of the noblest projects that ever was laid before a Nation'. In 1803 he was again in the North, this time accompanied by William Jessop, his consulting engineer at Ellesmere, to recheck the costing and put preparatory work in hand. A fresh estimate added £120,000 to the original sum, and that was without the cost of land. Neither man expected to pay much for that. One wonders if a power of compulsory purchase existed and what they would have done if any owner had refused to have a canal dug through land for which, in the not so distant past, gallons of Clan blood had been passionately spilt. Colonel MacDonnell of Glengarry, a brave and arrogant chief, came near to doing so. Though he had sold quantities of prime timber to the Canal Commissioners, he was extremely loath to have 'smoking steam-vessels' puffing through his grounds. They symbolised a new age that offended his feudal nature. He resolved, therefore, not to sell his privacy cheaply. He rejected one offer from the Commissioners in 1811 and insisted that another, made two years later, be taken to arbitration. In due course he was awarded £10,000 in compensation, much more than the land was worth, but his resentment still smouldered. It was fanned into sudden flame when a canal workers' boat ventured too close upon his view. With splendid autocracy he armed thirty of his retainers, scattered the Commissioners' men and seized their vessel as a reprisal. As a member of a proud, ultra-conservative, anachronistic breed that, though dying, will not lie down, he has my sneaking regard.

In 1804 Napoleon was Emperor, and Spain joined in the war against Great Britain. The military uses to which the Canal might be put became paramount and Telford was asked to estimate for new specifications. These consisted in lengthening and widening the locks so that 32-gun frigates might use the waterway. His quotation added £8000 to the bill, and now work began in earnest.

Like tunnellers who, for reasons of supply, begin at either end and meet in the middle, Telford set up his bases of operation at Corpach on the west and Clachnaharry on the east. At these places the sea basins would be built before the cutting of the canal into the hinterland. The resident engineer at Clachnaharry was Matthew Davidson, a tough, literate, abrasive master mason from Langholm who had worked as Telford's superintendent on a famous aqueduct. Davidson's opposite number at Corpach was John Telford (unrelated). The overall project was administered jointly by the Caledonian Canal Commissioners and the Commissioners for Roads and Bridges, whose members included the Speaker of the House of Commons and the Chancellor of the Exchequer. At ground level, so to speak, there was a contractor for all the mason work who employed two foremen at either end.

Clachnaharry soon became a hive of industry. Workshops, storehouses and huts for the labour force were springing up like mushrooms. A quarry for rubble was opened nearby; another, for its superior cutting stone, was dug at Redcastle, across the Beauly Firth; and a sloop was under construction at Kessock which would ship the stone to the site. Soundings were being made in the Firth to determine the best channel to the big Canal Basin. Huge quantities of timber were cut locally and on Lochness-side, and prime Baltic Pine imported via Aberdeen. Much of this was used in the fabrication of innumerable tip trucks and open wagons into which excavated material would be loaded. Though of varying construction, back-tilting or side-tilting, each had one thing in common, a capacity of one cubic yard. This was the measure on which piecework payment was made. Pay was adjusted according to the nature of the material; 6d. for earth, 2/– for hard rock at Corpoch, and so on. A labourer's time was valued at 1/6d. a day. It was more in England, an unfair discrepancy that existed for many years. At the same time it must be admitted that the Highland labourer was an awkward man. Fiercely individual as a result of his

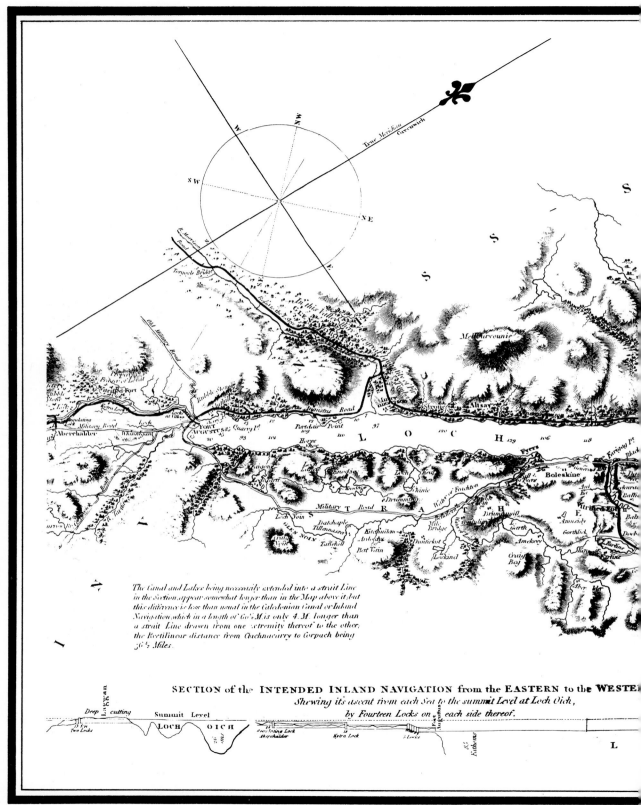

An early 19th-century map of Loch and Canal

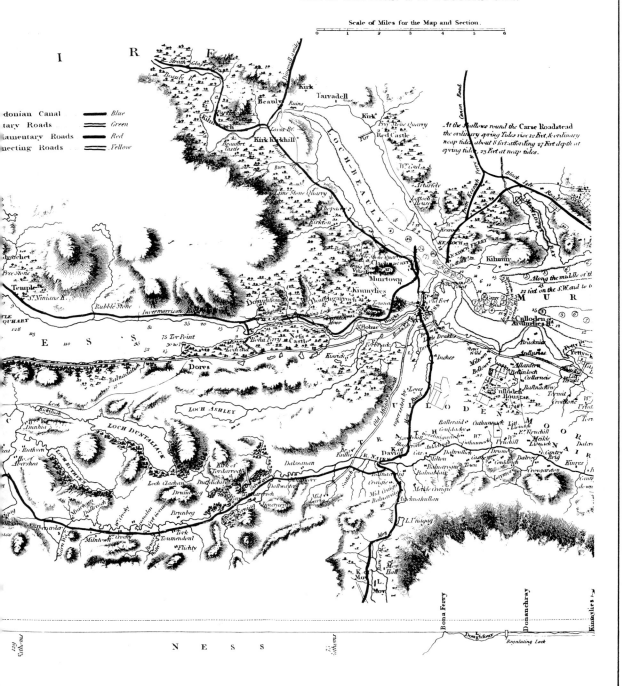

CALEDONIAN CANAL or INLAND NAVIGATION

From the EASTERN to the WESTERN SEA.

Scale of Miles for the Map and Section.

0   1   2   3   4   5   6

environment and culture, he did not take kindly to being organised or instructed. The seasonal demands of fishing, sowing and reaping, that had always been his mainstay, made him a temporary deserter in times of peace or war. The land, or the sea, was the ever-demanding mistress, and at her call all other considerations were put aside. Over the next nineteen years Thomas Telford was to learn this to his cost.

By the summer of 1804 there were almost a hundred men in the Clachnaharry basin, and soon the time came to break out into the open land of Kinmylies. To instruct his local labourers in the special use of pick and shovel Telford had imported seasoned veterans from other contracts. Many masons came from Wales but many others, hearing of the work, descended upon Clachnaharry from all directions. National changes took time to reach the north but with the building of the Caledonian Canal the Industrial Revolution came to Inverness-shire.

The deep trench of the Canal edged slowly westward against expected and unexpected difficulties. The shale and shingle, dumped by the long-vanished ice and now heaped up to form banks, was so porous that puddling with clay had to be resorted to. This process, not unlike wine making, was done by stamping mixed clay and sand into the gravel to the depth of two to three feet. It was necessarily slow and costly but there was no alternative. Failure to treat 'safe' sections in this way sometimes brought embarrassing outcomes, as when two families had to leave their homes in the Bught or the Provost of Inverness had his cellar flooded.

By the end of 1805 the canal cutters were working as far east as Dunain, three miles from Inverness. Here a major problem existed and it was some years before it was resolved. The line of the canal was planned to pass between the esker (a ridge of sand and gravel) of Torvean and the River Ness and the gap was so narrow that the situation called for major topographical surgery. It was further aggravated by the old Inverness to Fort Augustus road which passed close under the unstable flanks of the steep little hill. Telford's resolution of this complexity was characteristically bold. He left Torvean alone, gave the river a strong nudge to the south and resited the road, over three miles of it, to the north west of the esker. The great embankment, rooted in the former bed of the river, is over half a mile long, and laced with broom and whin which Telford first had planted to secure the soil. Sadly, for those who remember its virgin state, a license to rape pretty little Torvean has been in force for some years now, and the thin ridge is being steadily demolished for the sake of its gravel.

When Matthew Davidson died in 1819 the first stretch of canal, from the North Sea to Loch Ness, had been open for a year. Davidson was held in the highest regard by the Commissioners. Telford was the general but he had been the executive officer in the field with the widest powers of decision. Against great natural difficulties he had built the great sea basin at Clachnaharry, wound the coils of his canal around the obstacles of hill and river, dug thousands of tons of mud from Loch Dochfour and closed the thick artery of the River Ness with a weir of solid stone. At Muirtown he had raised a staircase of locks, and a single one at Dochgarroch whose essential function was to prevent overspill into the Ness Valley when the Loch rose after heavy rain.

Closing the weir at Dochfour and thus charging the canal with water led to an increase in Loch Ness's surface level of no less than nine feet. This added some 5500 million gallons to its capacity and meant that Telford's cast-iron lock-gates were, in effect, holding back around 24 million tons of water! A sobering thought, indeed, when one remembers that more than once in its short history impacts on the gates by rogue ships, or simple structural failure, have threatened populated areas with catastrophic inundation.

It is good that Matthew Davidson, whose immaculate masonry has stood the test of time, should have lived just long enough to see the east end of the canal operational. Telford's policy had been to postpone the construction of the flight of locks at Fort Augustus until this was established. But as early as 1813 the River Oich had been evicted from its ancient channel and relocated to the north, in order to avoid rock cutting and to keep the line of the canal as straight as possible, and two years later a total length of four miles had been cut. The labouring hosts required for this had caused the little Loch-side village to burst at the seams; men were lodged everywhere, in a hearty foretaste of the Bed-and-Breakfast boom of today.

Cutting through the glacial and alluvial desposits that underlay the peat between Fort Augustus and Loch Oich was relatively easy; finding natural foundations for the locks of Cullochy and Kytra, with their solid masonry and 50-ton gates, was a different matter. It was some time before a fold of rock was found beneath the canal at Kytra, and fortunately an outcrop of the granitic gneiss that paves the glen floor here extruded near by. The same was true at Cullochy, but it took even longer to find, in fact it was 1821, the eleventh hour, before the lock building there was complete. Over all this section the living spectre of the irate Glengarry, whose land it was, did nothing at all to bless the work.

These were the years of the Luddite riots when nervous men saw machines as enemies of their employment, but on the Caledonian Canal the great pumping engines were a sure guarantee of it. A gaunt stone building, that in 1816 housed a 36 h.p. pump, still stands near the admirable little Fort Augustus museum. Without the suck and spew of its powerful occupant – it could throw out water at the rate of 6000 gallons a minute – the excavators would not have been able to work twenty feet below Loch Ness's surface. The masons, when their turn came, required an even greater degree of dryness, for quick-setting cement was a thing of the future and their sand/lime mixture would have readily dispersed in water. Two more pumps were brought in for their benefit with a total force of over 60 h.p. So the great stone staircase rose, tier upon tier, until in 1817 Telford claimed that 'The most arduous and uncertain portion of this work at Fort Augustus has been accomplished'. His satisfaction, we may believe, was shared by his workers with spirits sharpened by competition between rival gangs and the enlivening spur of payment by results.

The Caledonian Canal was opened in October 1822. A steam yacht carrying Charles Grant (for the Canal Commissioners) and some interested landed proprietors left Muirtown at 11 a.m. on the 23rd and reached Fort Augustus seven hours later. At every point their progress had been marked by triumphant and congratulatory noises – shouts, cheers, the firing of guns and the music of a militia band – and further boardings by potentates and men of rank along the way. The party spent the night at the Fort and made an early start at 6 a.m. This uncivilised hour had not been lightly chosen; it was feared that the despotic Glengarry might choose the occasion to mount a demonstration or, knowing his hatred of steam vessels, even an armed confrontation. However, no such thing happened; instead the Chief came on board and later, at the celebrations in Fort William, he proposed three toasts – to whom, or what, is not recounted – before retiring to bed. Few were so abstemious; almost two score toasts were drunk by the gentlemen, while whisky flowed like water among canal workers and townspeople alike. This moment of mutual good feeling between the Highlanders and their English paymasters seems a symbolic interment of the hatchet that had spilled so much blood less than eighty years before.

For the first few years after its opening the Canal fell far short of its economic targets. The inflation which followed the end of the Napoleonic Wars had distorted the costs of construction and all the time unexpected expenses had to be met. Wages, especially, had soared by as much as 50% and amounted to well over half of the total budget, but almost all of this money went into Highland pockets with a consequent improvement in living standards. Another lasting benefit to the area resulted from the £4000 spent on Great Glen roads and bridges. Telford's fine old bridge at Invermoriston, now safely preserved, is an outstanding example. Others have vanished or have fallen into sad decay after more than a century of active life. He made massive improvements to what is now the A82 and from the early 19th century until its reconstruction in 1931–1933 this winding way followed every intimate crease in the hillside and crossed every burn at right angles. Its bounding walls and the outline of its track, now bristly with scrub birch and hazel, can still be seen in innumerable places, as can the tumbled remains of some of its narrow, compact bridges. It is an indictment of this disrespectful age that some of these unique stone monuments are now used as dumping grounds for domestic rubbish.

In the 165 years since its opening the Caledonian Canal has had a chequered history. Physical and financial problems existed from the start. In 1825 the

Commissioners found it necessary to double tonnage rates but some thrifty skippers were still prepared to risk the passage of the Pentland Firth for the modest saving of the extra 2/7d. a ton. All the time, steam-driven boats were getting larger and more powerful; their size precluded them from using the Canal and also made the Pentland route less hazardous. In the same year a massive leak developed at Dunaincroy, near Dochgarroch, which was eventually stopped by lining almost 600 yards of the bed and sides with woollen cloth into which thick clay was puddled. This original and resourceful measure was entirely successful, but it was expensive and caused the Canal to be closed for some time.

The next decade was a period of increasing mercantile trade and growing

The Locks at Fort Augustus

91

mobility. Steamships were carrying people regularly between Inverness and Glasgow, and the former town saw a considerable increase in its trade. This period of untroubled progress did not last long. In 1834 torrential rain swelled Loch Lochy until it was in danger of bursting through the Canal locks into the Corpach plain and this was only avoided by heroic efforts on the part of lock-keepers and steamer crews. It was a hazard that had to be dealt with and precautionary work was started at once. There was a more far-reaching calamity at Fort Augustus in 1837 when the wall of the lowest lock collapsed and jammed the gates. Many vessels in transit in the Canal had to turn back the way they had come.

This mishap coincided with the Commissioners' demand for a report on the Canal by its chief engineer. When compiled this was critical of the masonry work at the west end and suggested that the Canal had been opened prematurely for financial and prestigious reasons. It included proposals for expensive improvement but the project had already cost over £900,000 and had so far earned less than 1% annually on that sum. The Canal had leaked, it had flooded and now it was falling to pieces. Even as the report was under consideration more lock walls fell in at Banavie and Corpach. It was now on the cards that the Commissioners might decide to cut their losses and close the whole thing down.

It is fortunate that so weighty a decision could not be taken lightly. Further reports and opinons were sought from the Institute of Civil Engineers and a Select Committee of the House of Commons was set up in 1839. The business was debated in all its aspects and five years later Parliament gave the go-ahead for sweeping renovations. In 1844, 1500 men with horses and machinery were working along the Canal. It reopened in 1847 and Prince Albert gave it his royal blessing as he went through it in the screw steamer *Fairy*. Two years later it successfully withstood the memorable flood which destroyed the old stone bridge at Inverness.

In 1873 the widowed Queen Victoria took time off from her interminable mourning to follow the shade of her husband through the locks. She expressed admiration for the engineering workmanship but found travelling on the Canal 'very tedious' although the sight of men running 'round and round to move the windlasses' is said to have raised a royal smile. By then the passenger trade along the Canal was well established. The paddle steamers *Glengarry* and *Gondolier* were familiar sights as they churned their way down the Loch with calls at Glenurquhart, Inverfarigaig, Foyers, Invermoriston and Fort Augustus before going on to Fort William. The voyages of the *Lochiel* and the *Lochness* were restricted to within the Loch but they carried mail as well as passengers to and from the villages, while other boats worked between Inverness and Glasgow, and from as far south as Liverpool. There was strong competition between the companies involved.

As a boy, in the early 30s, I first remember the *Gondolier*. My father had sailed in her many years earlier. He was wont to recall with nostalgic relish the journey between Glasgow and Inverness, where he schooled for a while at the former Inverness College. He spoke of 'breakfasts on board of ham and eggs, sausages and bacon, or fresh herring' and 'of teas with the captain seated at the head of a tastefully decorated saloon'. The Captain was still alive in 1940, retired after having sailed over Loch Ness no fewer than 20,000 times. He had outlived the *Gondolier* which died honourably, intentionally scuttled in Scapa Flow to prevent the entry of U Boats. Her sister ship *Glengarry*, had been broken up thirteen years earlier; having reached the age of 83 she was claimed to be one of the world's oldest steamers.

The Caledonian Canal has always remained in public ownership and has never been made to pay. There are many villainous and wasteful purposes to which the taxpayer's money is put and the small debit on this canal is money well spent. But successive governments have not seen it like that. In 1906–1908 a Royal Commission decided against plans for improvement and maintenance, and the same fate awaited a somewhat grandiose proposal for its enlargement in 1921. Yet during the First War it was used extensively for military traffic (on which no dues were paid) and in the same period vast numbers of fishing boats travelled along it in safety from coast to coast. Again, in the Second War, it was a national asset of no small value. Only in 1958 did the Bowes Committee of Enquiry officially state what had long been obvious, that 'the waterway is a social service' and as such should be retained and properly looked after. Elaborate plans to modernise the lockgate machinery began in 1959 and by 1968 all the gates on the Canal were operated by hydraulic power. In the mid-70s the canal, which had been in existence for over 150 years, began to show its age. At Muirtown the owner of a cabin cruiser had a narrow escape when a lockgate failed behind his boat. At Laggan a wall collapsed and blocked the waterway. These were symptoms of a general deterioration but this time help was immediate and unstinted. The repair bill was estimated at over £900,000, as much (though not in real terms) as the whole canal had cost to build under Telford's management.

Nowadays, following a universal trend, the main activity of the canal is leisure though many fishermen still prefer it to the vicious conjunction of winds and tide in the Pentland Firth. In summer days the long surface of Loch Ness is dotted with the innumerable white shapes of cabin cruisers. Water-buses and *Scot II*, the former canal tug which replaced its forerunner *Scot I* in 1931, carry their daily quota of sightseeing passengers on to the Loch, and between places on it. All trips include a close glance at the old stone castle of Urquhart.

Telford, we are told, was a kindly man and I am sure he would have enjoyed the light-hearted purposes to which his 'whole great work' is being put. The poem, from which these words are taken, was written by his friend Robert Southey and is inscribed on a plaque mounted at Clachnaharry. Telford was also a conservationist ahead of his time, with a careful eye for the look of the countryside. At no point in its many miles are the reaches of the Canal offensive to the eye; in places they add an interest, even a fascination, to the natural background. What 20th-century man has done, by or around the Canal and its linking lochs, is a different story.

As a lifelong railway enthusiast I have often wondered how a track might have been built along the north-west side of Loch Ness. Merely an academic question now, it could have become a fact but for the bitter rivalry that existed between two railway companies. In 1865 the Highland Railway owned networks in the north and east while the North British Railway had its stronghold in the south west. Cut-throat competition ensured that any hint of expansion by one company towards the other's territory was instantly countered in the courts.

Matters came to a head in 1884. Slyly acting through a subsidiary – the Glasgow and North-Western Railway – the North British proposed to build a line from Glasgow to Inverness, via Loch Lomond, Rannoch Moor, the Pass of Glencoe and the Great Glen. It was a grandiose project, with some good thinking behind it, but the Bill was defeated in Parliament on the grounds, put forward by the Highland Railway, that there was insufficient traffic to go round. Be that as it may, a railway through the Great Glen to Inverness would certainly have robbed the Canal Commissioners of some of their dues.

The proposal was disinterred a few years later but this time the North British prudently excluded from the proposal their rival's *bête noire*, the Great Glen link with Inverness, that town being strongly defended Highland Railway territory. Now it was the North British's turn to win and the railway, as far as Spean Bridge, was opened in 1894. But the big issue was still unresolved. After heated argument a temporary truce was called and it was mutually agreed that neither the North British nor the Highland would press for the Great Glen route for the next ten years. But this truce didn't hold. By 1897 three separate Bills were brought in Parliament, one each by the main contestants and the third by the newly formed Invergarry & Fort Augustus Railway which, a year earlier, had been sanctioned to lay a track between Spean Bridge and Fort Augustus. The gap was closing – Inverness was hardly thirty miles away – and the tempo of litigation increased. In the same year an independent company applied for permission to take a light railway through from Inverness Station to Lochend. It gained little support from any quarter and the idea was eventually abandoned but on paper at least it was the nearest the two railheads ever got to each other. Meanwhile the Highland Railway had gained the approval of the Commons to push through to Fort William but the Lords, having the final say, vetoed it.

The Invergarry & Fort Augustus Railway was now on its own and sadly under-capitalised. They had underestimated the cost of laying their line along the south-east side of the Great Glen where the steep slopes are seamed by many watercourses and bulging with ridges. By the time the Company had dug culverts and banked in hollows most of their working capital was gone. What was left was insufficient to buy rolling stock. The I.F.A.R., in this somewhat ridiculous situation, went first to

Fort Augustus station, with the shadows of waiting carriages on the left.

the North British, then to the West Highland, desperately seeking the best bargain with the fewest strings attached. This led to further fierce dispute between the rival companies while the new line remained idle. Eventually it opened in 1903. The Highland Railway had agreed to run it for a minimum of ten years, and the North British took it over from them for a further four. At last the two companies had agreed to a state of peaceful coexistence on the understanding that neither would infringe the status quo. The great gap between Inverness and Fort Augustus was fixed forever.

From the main station at Fort Augustus a line had run to a pier on Loch Ness, a terminus at which the steamers used to call. It crossed the Canal by a hand-operated swing-bridge and the River Oich by a viaduct. In the summers only, up until 1907, trains ran as far as the Pier Station, but in that year the service ended, as the direct result of the refusal to allow the Highland Railway to run its own steam-boats on Loch Ness. When this had been proposed, two years earlier, Messrs. David MacBrayne and the Invergarry Railway Co. had combined in their separate objec-tions to the plan. The mile-long track was never used again and quickly fell into decay; eventually the rails were lifted, the swing-bridge taken away and the super-structure of the viaduct dismantled.

The pillars of the viaduct still stand as a reminder of this ill-starred project. As a child on holiday in Fort Augustus I once found some chocks among the rusted, overgrown permanent way and took them to our home in Norfolk where, in an empty loft, I had made a small collection of railway miscellanea. My obsession with railways was perhaps genetic in that my great grandfather had been a friend and associate of the famous engineer Isambard Kingdom Brunel.

The amputation of this limb of the Invergarry–Fort Augustus line did no more than delay the death of the main body. It was merged with the L.N.E.R. after 1921 and passenger trains continued to run on weekdays until 1933. By then it was fast becoming uneconomic and services were suspended; a single coal train ran weekly for a few more years.

And that was the end of the railway presence on Loch Ness. A dog-in-the-manger attitude in business prevented the dream of a useful and highly scenic line from coming to fruition. Even if the Loch-side link had become a reality I suppose it would have fallen to the Beeching axe, but what a wonderful challenge it would have been to such dedicated enthusiasts as those who rescued, and ran so well, the Grantown-on-Spey to Boat of Garten line.

6 Trees and Temperature

I N THE north of Scotland birch and aspen were the first settlers after the melting of the ice. Undemanding as to their habitat, wind resisting, tough and fast growing they thrust their wiry roots into every nook and cranny of the new land. Further south the conifers were at first in difficulties, often shaded out by the wide canopies of broad-leaved species, but as they edged north their condition improved. Huge tracts of the Scottish Highlands were relatively soon covered in Scots Pine.

Later, except in the far north of the country, the oak began to establish itself in strength, sharing the glens and hillsides with the resident pine. In our Loch Ness area we can guess, from early records, how well both species succeeded. The Count of St. Pol in Flanders was probably aware of the excellent timber around the Loch when, in 1249, he ordered a ship to be built in Inverness to take him and his companions to the Crusades. This 'wonderful ship', the biggest built in the north, was fashioned out of oak and pine floated down the Loch and River Ness from the mouths of Glenurquhart and Glenmoriston. Rather later, in the 17th century, the Lairds of Grant supplied fine oak for the repair of Fortrose Cathedral, and in the 18th century huge quantities of oak were felled all around the Loch to fetch what were then enormous prices. Sir Ludovick Grant, indecisive in politics, was sharp enough in business; it was said that he sold a number of oak trees from Ruiskich for £1000 which was directly applied to the building of the new Castle Grant on Speyside. Over in Glenmoriston the laird took £2000 from his woodlands in 1760 and in 1784 the Laird of Aldourie wrote that he had marked a hundred fine oaks for felling. On the Ruiskich slope you can still see the crumbling, moss-clad, roughly hewn stumps of Sir Ludovick's oaks and in places even a whole specimen, bleached and barkless, propped on its limbs like a fearsome spider.

Loch Ness

Loch Ness today is ringed by woods and forests. Most of these are 'timber factories', as Wordsworth called them, planned by bureaucrats and planted by hand, which rise, rank upon rank, in soulless uniformity of form and colour, except where geometric strips of larch provide seasonal change of hue. Beneath their tightly compressed crowns mid-day is dusk and dusk is mid-night; in the brown gloom nothing grows and even the ants, their only residents, seem to go about their duties with bated breath in their swollen and obscene hills. There is an unusual silence within these wooden walls but it is the silence of the padded cell, a killing of sound rather than its absence, and when a pigeon or a lumbering capercaillie cracks some brittle, light-starved branch the noise is as sharp as a rifle shot and makes one jump in alarm. In places moss hangs loosely from tumbled trees or lies thickly upon the pine needles as if it were the grave clothes of dryads who have died from the effects of overcrowding on their free, volatile spirits.

These commercial forests on Loch Ness date back to 1919 when the Forestry Commission was formed with the object of ensuring that Britain would not have to rely on imported timber in the event of another major conflict. Its creation showed little faith in the promise that the recent bloody business was The War to end All Wars, and in the event the second one came too soon after the first to justify the Commission's primary *raison d'être*. In 1939 the growing trees were still much too small for anything but pit props and, once again, privately owned mature forests bore the full brunt of the demand.

In the year of its formation the Commission fued ground from its first chairman, Lord Lovat, at Inchnacardoch, just west of Fort Augustus. It was to become the earliest state owned forest in Scotland and some interest attaches to the fact that its northern edge encloses the Military Road from the Fort to Glenelg over which Boswell and Johnson rode in 1773. By 1924 the Commission had acquired all the steep hillside which extends from Fort Augustus to Bunloit, south of Glenurquhart, so hanging more than half the Loch's north-west side with strips of their monotonous dark green wallpaper. Beneath it the fine, wild, precipitous slope of native oak, ash, birch and hazel, complete with its varied and complex ecology, slowly vanished without trace. After the last war the Commission was again active in increasing its holdings around Loch Ness. They planted at the mouth of Glenurquhart where wartime fellings had stripped the slopes of fine, native pine and replaced it with densely sown fir, spruce and larch. Many of these trees were planted in such inaccessible ground that they seem to have been forgotten altogether.

This policy of 'plant and be damned' has been steadily modified since the War. Until 1958, 'the Commission's principal objective was to build up a strategic reserve of timber', but since then, 'the emphasis has moved towards economic and social objectives.' They have done well in providing good, healthy work in areas of

Lord Lovat, first chairman of the Forestry Commission

unemployment although the general movement towards increased mechanism has limited the growth of the workforce. Nowadays a man with a chainsaw can do the job of ten men with cross-cuts; horsemen have been replaced by overhead cables; lorries load themselves with enormous grabs; old men, retired from active lumbering, no longer peel pitprops in the yards. But this is a universal change which many see as 'progress', and some do not.

Fort Augustus: the Monastery in the foreground, the pillars that supported the old railway viaduct over the River Oich behind, and forestry as the backdrop

With a shorter working week and more money available a growing taste for outdoor activities has characterised the last few decades and the Commission has had the wisdom to make their forests much more attractive places. When they took over the privately owned forest of Inverfarigaig, for instance, they embarked on a plan that has had a most felicitous outcome. This, I think, is forestry which can be enjoyed by all. A stroll along one of their laid-out trails, beneath towering Sitka and Norway Spruce, massive Douglas Fir and the more delicate European larch, with birch and natural woodland never far away, leaves one with the satisfied feeling that here man has nature's interests at heart. The trails are well graded and

constructed so as to appeal to all, the young and the old, the firm and infirm; they all start at an exhibition centre, delightfully situated in a glade behind a beech hedge, which contains a wealth of local information. A pamphlet can be used in conjunction with numbered posts throughout the forest; everyone who comes will be a little wiser after a visit. The surroundings of this open-air classroom are extremely beautiful. Ornamental conifers, planted at the turn of the present century, form an avenue of cypress, red cedar and sequoia along the narrow road that climbs the Pass, over which hangs the birch-clad splinter of Dun Dearduil, Deirdre's likely retreat. Lower down, on the shattered walls of the gorge, warped saplings cling like green cobwebs in this haunt of ravens and buzzards.

As a boy it was one of my haunts too. My young friends and I knew each inch of the girdling rock face, every pool in the boisterous river. It had, and still has, a special charm for me which the Forestry Commission's leisure developments have done nothing at all to spoil. Recently I sat alone in the warm, August sun on a heathery rock at the Gorge Viewpoint. I looked across at the crags opposite, and thought of the risks we had taken and the fierce pleasure we found in doing so. We were fortunate that nothing serious ever happened to us. Poor Dr James Bryce, a distinguished geologist, was less lucky: a memorial further up the Pass commemorates his death in a fall from the crags in 1877.

A glance at the map of the Loch will show that it is now almost surrounded by extensive blocks of conifers. Natural woodlands, made up largely of alder, ash, birch, willow, hazel, aspen, oak and rowan exist in quantity only between Fort Augustus and Foyers above that stretch of roadless, uninhabited shoreline which defeated both General Wade and commercial tree planters alike. Today it is Loch Ness's only wilderness area, hardly changed since the glacial melt-waters deepened the faults which carry the streams of Doe, Knockie and Kemp to the Loch. Inland from it a sea of young conifers is beginning to blur and spoil the dramatic contours of Tor Paiteag and other small, sharp hills.

Loch Ness can boast of some remarkable specimen trees, notably in the mouth of Glenurquhart. Within the policies of the once grand Balmacaan House (demolished as unsafe some years ago, and now a pile of crumpled walls and debris) is a vastly impressive stand of conifers. Among them is one of the two largest Grand Firs known in cultivation; and a Douglas Fir and a Giant Sequoia which are among the biggest in Britain. If the performance of these trees is in any way comparable to that of their Canadian and Californian cousins they will continue to grow for many years, since in terms of total life span they are no more than big children. The Sequoia is also found in the Glen outside this preserve, its brown punchbag bark and expansive bole dominant in more than one village garden, while noble examples of the Grey and Lombardy poplar are conspicuous features of the north slope of the glen.

Over: the specimen trees at Balmacaan

Another notable woodland thrives in the alluvium at the confluence of the Coiltie and the Enrick. Here is a habitat exactly suited to the needs of the Alder and that singular tree, whose timber blushes to the colour of thin blood when it is severed from its root, does full justice to it. A struggle through its tangled undergrowth with hectic jumps across the turgid channels that ooze towards the river is like a journey through some primaeval swamp.

The Hazel is widespread around the Loch and particularly below Abriachan where it thrives on the free-draining granite-formed soil. The extensively coppiced clumps bear witness to the many uses to which its wood has traditionally been put. Nowhere will you find a fully developed tree. Once, years ago, I built a sawmill on the steep Abriachan hill, facing the Loch, with the object of making fir posts from timber felled on the higher moorland. A strong local demand for hazel produce in a variety of forms was soon evident; my man and I were often engaged in seeking out suitable shoots with a bit of the stock attached which were then fashioned into elegant walking sticks or practical crooks with painstakingly polished handles. Bundles of shoots were also taken for fencing or sheep stakes. Once we had a visit from a whimsical man who needed a stick for his water divining. He searched for many hours and eventually found what he wanted; on leaving with his twisted rod he told us, straight faced, that only certain trees contained the special magic.

In places where land cleared of conifers has not yet been replanted natural regeneration is doggedly taking place. Of the billions of tree seeds gusted by the wind or carried by other agencies only a handful find earth to root in but already a complex habitat is forming. At first, when the tiny trees compete with thorn and weed, the pippit, winchat and willow warbler, along with less common birds, establish a home. Later, as the growing trees close in, the song thrush, blackbird and chaffinch predominate. The siskin likes the shadowed floors of forests and sometimes, beneath the great Scots fir of an earlier generation, you will find the crossbill using his special skill to open swollen cones in search of succulent seeds.

Near the mouths of the Loch Ness glens the woodpecker hammers with power and resonance. Cuckoos, in their season, are choosy visitors, local and selective; we hardly hear them at all on our side of Glenurquhart but in places not far away they are loud and persistent. Year after year, however, our special friends, the house martins, return to their nests under our eaves in May where, after throwing out a few opportunist sparrows, they breed their young families. Buzzards, mewing like cats, circle the moors and higher fields and are often seen perching on roadside trees.

The peregrine falcon is a familiar sight to those who know where to look in the vicinity of Fort Augustus, and for a time there were an aerobatic pair on Mealfuarvonie, but they have gone. That mountain's bare, old head is loud with ravens and on the edge of its highest point ptarmigan burst from cover like shell fragments if you approach; in winter they are dressed all in white, in the fashion of camouflaged alpine troops. Until recent years eagles resided on Mealfuarvonie but they, like the falcons, have left. In my submission, jet aircraft, that go up and down the Loch and sometimes over the back of the mountain, have driven them away. On the concave south east face the noise of their engines is deafening and sends a tremor through the air that can dislodge small stones and heather twigs.

In the growing forests the pine marten is on the increase but even if that increase were tenfold his shyness and swiftness – he can outpace the eye! – would never make his a familiar face. The roe deer, on the other hand, seems to be gaining in boldness. I often come within whispering distance of them during my walks around the Loch. Once, in an Autumn evening with the light fading from the sky, I turned a corner of path in the Ruiskich Wood to find a fine, sturdy young animal not ten yards from me. He stood absolutely still with his big, brown eyes fixed on something near my feet. It was my labrador dog, Brutus, who, equally still, was returning the roe's stare with a kind of speculative candour. Only when I snapped the lead onto the dog's collar was the spell broken. The roe sniffed audibly, turned on its hooves and wandered away among the darkening trees.

The first impression a visitor gains of Loch Ness is of its extreme size. Loch Lomond has a larger surface area but its islands and twisted shoreline break it up. Here the uniform topography of the parallel shores, with hardly a headland and never a natural island to confuse the eye, allows one to take in the whole of it at a single, uncomplicated glance. What lies beneath this two-dimensional image is even more impressive. Huge numbers of fish – notably the salmon, brown trout and sea trout, with a variety of other species – live in its depths, and innumerable eels. Some of these eels are up to six feet long and in the murky darkness deep down they are pure white in colour. On the surface ducks and, less often, otters are present and in their more playful moments have been known to impersonate the Loch Ness Monster (Nessie), whose meteoric rise to world fame I shall discuss in another chapter.

Owing to the influence of the south-west wind and the fact that at this narrow neck of Scotland the North Sea and the Atlantic are only about seventy miles apart Loch Ness has several individual climates. The most marked feature of these weather patterns is the variation in rainfall. The annual precipitation for Drumnadrochit is thirty-nine inches, about twelve inches greater than that of Inverness. As a general rule the rainfall increases by an inch for every mile you travel west along the Loch although the graph line rises most steeply as you pass through the 'Cluanie Curtain', the meteorological nickname for an imaginary line that runs roughly along the east/west watershed. Foyers, on the west side of the 'curtain', is only six miles from Drumnadrochit but its annual rainfall is fifty-eight inches. When a wet wind blows from the Atlantic Mealfuarvonie, opposite Foyers, is frequently dark and lowering, often mist covered, while the woods and fields of lower Glenurquhart are bathed in sunshine. Cannich, ten miles from here, is very much wetter; the loaded rain clouds break against its high mountain ranges.

A strong south-westerly, or less often a north-easterly, wind soon wrinkles the twenty-four miles of water into short, steep waves with narrow troughs which pound the shores at Lochend and Fort Augustus; the swash and backwash roll and grind the pebbles with a harsh rumbling sound. When such a wind reaches storm force the whole surface of the Loch crawls beneath a single unbroken sheet of spray. Side winds, blowing at right angles to the Loch, use the glens and gullies like open windows and form weird, racing shadows as they touch the surface.

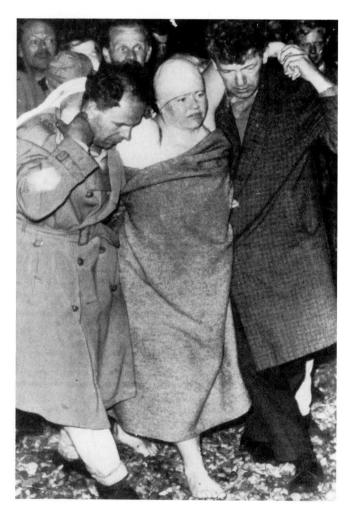

Brenda Sherratt, the first person to swim the length of the Loch.

The water temperature, by reason of continuous convection, is almost constant throughout the year, but never comfortable for swimming. Nonetheless remarkable long-distance swims have been made along the length of the Loch since the pioneer performance of Miss Brenda Sherratt, an eighteen-year-old girl who covered the distance in 18½ hours in July 1966. I believe that it has also been done both ways without the swimmer touching bottom. These feats must surely rank among the most severe tests to destruction that humans can devise for themselves; masochism at its most impressive.

In the shadow of such giants of the game I hesitate to mention my own modest crossing of the Loch, and only do so in order to describe, in microcosm, the feelings and reactions of my bolder betters. At the time I was a foolhardy boy of 16 who dabbled in a number of sports without being master of any one of them. I was going through my swimming period and had achieved distances of two or three miles in sea water so I looked upon the one and half mile crossing from Abriachan to Dores without much trepidation. My father insisted on following me in a boat but I proposed that he, with a local boatman, kept his distance.

It was a warm, late August day when I waded into deep water below the old Abriachan pier and saw my toes vanish in water which is as dark as beer. My God, it was cold! Exploratory dips during the previous few days had told me that, but then I had used a vigorous crawl over a few hundred yards. I had never been able to sustain that stroke for much further and now it was to be the breaststroke for the next hour or so. In the event it took me seventy-five minutes. Long before I reached the half-way mark most of the blood in my unoiled body had retreated to its core. I had the feeling that the calf muscle in my left leg was bunching up with cramp but the anaesthetic cold had changed agony to mere discomfort. Between strokes I held up a hand whose fingers were white as snow and looked unnaturally thin, like those of a skeleton. From time to time I twisted my head for a glance at my anxious father, but dared neither to wave nor shout in case he interpreted my gestures as signals of defeat. 'And not waving, but drowning', as Stevie Smith would say in about twenty-five years' time.

At about the time that the tree-clad crown of Tor Point showed that I was entering Dores Bay I became aware of a strange sensation. Until then my body had lacked the buoyancy that one expects to find even in fresh water. I could certainly not have floated in it and there was, in truth, an almost sinister feeling of being sucked down. Then, within moments, I found myself riding quite effortlessly on the surface while at the same time there was a delicious increase in the temperature coming up from below. I suppose that it was only in the order of one or two degrees but it was like a kind friend's welcome to his fire on a churlish night. I wallowed in voluptuous pleasure while my sluggish brain deduced that I had chanced upon a thermal current connected with the shallower water of Dores Bay. It did not last;

within minutes I was swimming out of it into water which, after the brief respite, felt even colder. As I left this warm bubble I was surprised to find that its perimeter was slowly rotating; I had to make a conscious effort to keep Dores Pier, my intended finishing post, straight ahead of me, for the area in which I swam, about an acre in extent, was gently but inexorably turning clockwise and deflecting me towards the west. Neither this, nor an off-shore breeze that had risen unkindly, served to deter me at this late stage, for the Dores shore was no longer far away and growing larger with each stroke.

When, a short time later, I crawled onto the slippery pebble beach I found that I could hardly get to my feet. I was too cold even to shiver; parts of my body were bluey white, other parts salmon pink. When my father landed nearby with towels and my clothes I was unable to dry myself without help. But although my fingers and toes remained bloodless for some time, even after a brisk dash along the shore, a flask of coffee laced with brandy fuelled my triumph and set off a boastful recital that went on for hours.

So Loch Ness is cold but not cold enough to freeze. When the temperature in the glens falls as low as −15°C or even less in winter nights only the pebbles on the beach are ice clad. After such nights a thick mist forms as the warmer moisture meets the heavy freezing air and persists until the sun dispels it. More than once I have climbed Mealfuarvonie for the pleasure of rising out of this cold grey mist onto a sunlit summit. Despite the fact that it is two thousand feet above the Loch the temperature may be as much as ten degrees higher there. This is adiobatic inversion, when the layer of air next to the earth's surface is cooler than an over-lying layer. It is not connected with the sun's heat and is the reversal of the normal situation.

After prolonged periods of Summer or Autumn heat Inverness, in common with most of the country's east coast, is subject to dense banks of haar, another condition associated with temperature differences between sea and air. In our area when the wind is north-easterly this extends inland along the Loch, thinning as it goes. Here, in Drumnadrochit, we are fortunate in that we often see the sun by early afternoon while Inverness may well remain under the chilly grey cloud throughout the day. Fort Augustus at the same time is even better served, often escaping the haar completely. On an annual basis this tends to balance the sun-shine position between the two ends of the Loch.

With calm air and a high barometer the mouths of glens Urquhart and Moriston and Fort Augustus have frequently recorded very high temperatures from May to August. In 1984 31°C was registered in the latter month. Drumnadrochit, for a single day, was the hottest place in Europe. It has never been the coldest; the shore-side climate of Loch Ness is equable and free from the unpleasant excesses that often affect places both north and south of us. Though Springs are certainly short by English standards, Autumns are long, mostly mild, and invariably glorious. The great mirror of the Loch is extremely sensitive to every variation in hue of the sky above it and when the ultramarine of high Summer has been thinned to paler blue it is as if the surplus colour has been added to the water. In this season the woodlands blaze with splashes of russet, fading green, and red while the forests stand in their immutable black-green dressing, stolid and silent, as though envious of their deciduous cousins.

In average years snow does not linger long in the mouths of the glens. After a light fall the permanent effects of warm convection currents from the great mass of the Loch is very apparent. On the low lying ground this higher temperature, compressed in the glens by the cold air above, melts the snow rapidly while on the topmost fields and moors, only a few hundred feet higher, it can linger for days.

On the whole, then, our Loch Ness winters are not unusually severe but even the most equable climate has a trick or two up its sleeve. The 27th of January 1978, an ordinary dark and windless winter's day, issued in a spell of most dramatic weather. It began to snow that night and it continued throughout the next day, falling quietly, steadily and unhurriedly, until all the glen's topography, natural and artificial, was covered evenly to the depth of a foot or more. The absence of wind coupled with a thawing temperature ensured that the snow balanced and grew on trees and cables until they could stand its weight no more. By the second evening things began to give way. Our lights having failed my wife and I went early to bed; there we listened to the snow avalanching down our roof, carrying some gutters with it, and saw, through closed curtains, the flashes of the Hydro-Electric cables as they parted under the strain.

The next day, the 29th, was a Sunday and none the better for it. In our drive the smaller trees were bent double like old, tired men, their lower limbs pressed down into several feet of snow. It was sad to find that our greenhouse roof had collapsed and that our numerous geraniums had been frozen, or cut to pieces by falling glass. An amorphous mound outside the house was all that could be seen of my car. The telephone system, which had manfully resisted the attack, conceded defeat by dusk.

While our position, a hundred yards from the main road and half a mile from the village, was uncomfortable, it was a grim time for people, especially the old and infirm, who lived on the higher ground or at the end of impenetrable roads. The authorities acted quickly and laid on a helicopter which made several errands of mercy. One of our friends, having made his cross in the snow, was lifted from his eyrie and carried, like a stricken eagle, to Inverness. It is a measure of the isolation caused by the storm that, in a village where each man knows his neighbour's business better than his own, such news remained untold for several days.

The huge canopy of snow now caused a fall in the air temperature and a heavy frost set in. This delayed the clearing of roads and the repair of cables; it was the 4th February before power was restored. About a week later I climbed Mealfuarvonie in magnificent, glittering frost. I have known this small mountain for over fifty years – I was twelve when I went there first – but this was the single occasion on which I found it to be 'in condition' for serious winter climbing. The higher trees in the Ruiskich Wood had been devastated by the snow fall. Some stood like ragged poles, their branches prised away from the trunks; others, thinner and more flexible, had their crowns pressed against the ground. It took me more than twice the customary time to find my way through this altered country, and in the deep, soft snow. But on the Lon na Fala, where one's steps are usually restrained by marsh and lanky heather, the snow was not soft; it was a white pavement, too solid even to show a footprint, and beyond it Mealfuarvonie, that most amiable of mountains, had become a formidable castle fortified by a shell of ice.

The delicate climb up the front, aided by two sticks in place of ice picks, is something I shall always remember, as were the long glissades down the gentler slopes to the west with my dog Brutus romping joyously behind me.

7   *The Modern Scene*

TOURISM AROUND Loch Ness, as in the Highlands as a whole, reached a peak in the 1960s and 1970s when hotel keepers built extra accommodation in the belief that the visiting geese would lay their golden eggs forever. It proved to be a false surmise. Disenchanted by low standards of hospitality which resulted from haste and greed, and lured away by cheaper holidays in the more certain sun, holiday-makers started to seek their pleasures elsewhere.

Now, in the 1980s, the business of entertaining guests remains a substantial concern from which many people derive their main or extra incomes. In Drumnadrochit the lodestone of the 'Official' Monster Exhibition attracts both trippers and the more seriously minded in vast numbers. In July and August our area is alive with tourists; from dawn until dusk the Loch-side resounds to the roar of cars and coaches filled with people of all nationalities. The A 82 road between Inverness and Fort Augustus must be one of the busiest in the country.

It was very different in 1935. The road had recently been improved; it had a well-made surface for its time but it was narrower than it is now, and there were some tight bends. As to the traffic, I have it in my diary that in August of that year I set out with a couple of friends to walk from Inverness to Brackla (where the New Clansman Hotel now stands) to explore the waterfall gorge there. With the fatuous exuberance of youth we decided to wave to every car that came towards us and to record the response. In our three-hour walk, taken at peak traffic time sixteen motorists drove east of whom twelve returned our salute. On the way home we had a fifty per cent success rate from eight cars going west. Today such a performance as ours would constitute a traffic hazard.

A lot of other things were different too. As we trudged round the sharp bend at the west end of Loch Dochfour our first view of the Loch would not have been interrupted by the cluster of council houses at Lochend. They were built not long after the last war and, while models of their kind, have an appearance of fragmented suburbia that clashes badly with the scenery. Aldourie Castle, or rather the present mansion which incorporates a 16th-century tower, has the contrived fairytale look so often associated with Victorian success. But it is more appropriate to its setting than the Lochend council house development. Two of Wade's galley's cannon are still there. On the steep pebble beach there used to be a machine for working stone, a rigid, lanky construction that was worth climbing for the view alone, especially on stormy days. It has vanished almost without trace and the boiler of its engine has long lain in deep water just off the shore. Of remarkable durability – they have hardly decayed in fifty years – are the skeleton prow and ribs of a wooden boat that rests on the shingle bottom nearby. The story goes that it was grounded after it had caught fire during an on-board party in the early part of this century. One of the crew, no doubt inspired by the spirits, plunged back into the water to rescue the most valuable thing he could think of, the ship's gramophone and records!

This merry tale contrasts with the dolorous events that once took place in Bona Castle (otherwise Caisteal Spioradain, see p. 45). Remnants of the stronghold that dominated the ford across the River Ness are concealed beneath a tree-capped mound which lies between the Canal and Abban Water, two hundred yards or so east of Bona Light-house. Not much can be left; a ruin long before the Canal was planned, its builders used much of the stone work and some of the foundations were submerged when the level of Loch Ness was raised by the weir at Dochfour. When I went there recently to refresh my memory I was struck by the way the tall, thin larch trees on the mound lean over towards the Canal. They extend beyond the canopy, like supplicating arms at the barred window of a dungeon. I was prompted by this fancy to enquire of Mr George Reid, the present owner of the light-house, if he had ever heard cries or groans. He smiled and pointed to bare places on the stems, where the wood was worn and polished, before telling me that on windy nights the trees rub together and make weird and frightening sounds. In a mood of whimsy I thought that the tree nymphs must be sympathetic to the spirits of the hostages who had died there so long ago.

Mr Reid is a geologist and a man of an enquiring mind. Soon he took me to a windblown tree and scooped up a handful of flint pebbles from beneath its root. He explained that flint does not exist locally and that these stones must have been brought from a great distance. He would not be surprised to find arrow and axe heads. All along the Lochend shore ancient human bones have been discovered as well as a beaker and a skull in a Bronze Age kist. These finds endorse the theory

that from Neolithic times onwards the Ness valley and adjacent hill slopes were well *Bona Light-house*
populated.

Science, which is usually concerned with the solution of mysteries, can sometimes create new ones in the process. A case in point was the detection by sidescan sonar of large round heaps of stone in forty feet of water just off Bona Light-house. When they were first observed in 1976 they were uncritically compared to Stonehenge, an extraordinary analogy. Allowing for the fact that the weir at Dochfour had raised the surface level of Loch Ness by nine feet, this assertion implied that neolithic circle builders had worked in thirty feet of water. Either that, or the Loch was lower then, but there is no evidence to support that idea. The mystery was solved when it was remembered that the *Prince Regent*, one of Telford's dredgers,

113

had dumped hundreds of tons of stone in Loch Ness, and put to final proof by a diver who compared some stones that he had lifted from the bottom to those in an old Canal quarry. It is a mercy that this truth was discovered before an Official Neolithic Exhibition took root near the site.

As we continued on our westward way in 1935 we would have passed the junction with the then rough and gravelly road that leads to Abriachan. This was once a crofting community, a fact remembered in the Croft Museum there and by the highly evocative book, *A Croft in the Hills* by Katherine Stewart. Some of the houses that were ruinous in those pre-war and immediate post-war years have been bought and renovated (some with help from the benevolent Highland Board) by people who are prepared to put up with difficult winter access for the sake of the magnificent view and a not too serious isolation. Abriachan is becoming sought-after and smart, the early symptoms of the disease of urbanism, and I fear it is contagious. Few places around the Loch are safe from the infection.

This area of Loch Ness-side is particularly rich in ancient memories. Killianan churchyard, between the Abriachan road end and the attractive commercial nursery garden, is the site of an early church dedicated to St Adamnan, the abbot of Iona and Columba's hagiographer. Here lies a graveslab which probably dates from the 14th century. Known only to the few, and hard to find in the dense bramble and hazel above the road, is a stone whose use was once central to an early form of trial marriage. Here the contracting couple would kneel and join their hands in a hollow carved in the stone, thereafter announcing to each other, and witnesses, that they were provisionally married for one year from that day. If in that time their mutual ardour cooled, and providing no child had been conceived, they were free to part with nothing lost except the girl's virginity. It seems to me to have been a sensible custom, refreshingly free from hypocrisy, which fully acknowledged the fact that in human relationships few things are more certain than change.

West of Abriachan village is Loch Laide, an almost circular sheet of water which contains a tiny crannog. Up until ten years ago it was a nesting place for the Slavonian Grebe but Forestry Commission plowings on the hill to the south-west have influenced the water table in a way which is discouraging to the birds. They have left and set up house in Loch Dochfour along with an even more exciting newcomer there, the Osprey. Moving west, through the denseness of the new forest, it is still possible to locate the ruins of Donald Fraser's 19th-century bothy. Fraser was called the 'King of the Smugglers' for good reason; from his stills in the area, so sited because of the unusual purity of the water, gushed gallons of fine duty-free whisky. His name is remembered with reverence.

The road from Abriachan down to Beauly bisects the ancient route from Inverness to Glenurquhart which was in regular use until the end of the 18th century when the 'Good' Sir James Grant, son of Ludovick Grant, the not so good

The Good Sir James

SIR JAMES GRANT OF GRANT BARONET,
B. 19ᵀᴴ MAY 1738.   M. JANUARY 1763.   D. 18ᵀᴴ FEBRUARY 1811.

The Brackla gorge

dissembler of the '45, promoted and completed a loch-side road. There is no modern continuation of the former way beyond Abriachan; the old road is just a rutted hill track, deeply etched in the peat and heather. The sketchy line of another road, which was put to much use by drovers in olden times, is still in evidence where it crosses the Inverness/Glenurquhart road in the hills above Lochend. This is the one that ran from Beauly and points south to Dores and Strathnairn, crossing the Ness by the Bona Ferry. It is said that Montrose and his army came this way after his siege of Inverness was raised by General Middleton in 1646.

We shall return to the Loch-side at Brackla where in 1935 there was a single house and an enormous and noteworthy specimen of the araucaria, or Monkey Puzzle. Up in the wood, below the devastated cliff face of which it was once a part, is the Clach an Fion, or Wine Stone, an enormous monolith, once supposed to be the largest in Scotland. This claim is open to question but the origin of its name is suggested by the remnants of a still which are scattered around amid the rocks. High above the Wine Stone the Brackla Burn spills down a red cliff into a narrow, umbrageous channel partly blocked by rocks. The penetration of this natural dungeon and the escape by its wooded left wall was then usually accomplished by rock and tree climbing and, if necessary, by swimming, and when we first settled in Drumnadrochit in 1960 it was a fine lark to invite unsuspecting friends there after a party and show them how it could be done. All agreed that it was a most sobering experience. But today Brackla is changed, for the better or worse according to one's taste. The araucaria has long since turned brown and died, and the New Clansman Hotel 'complex', which incorporates a berth for cabin cruisers and a calling point for a waterbus, now dominates the area. It is a testament to tourism, a supplier of the demands of the majority who pass this way and less egregious than some other buildings that have sprung up around the Loch. A few of these, indeed, are in astoundingly bad taste, and a minority such wretched anomalies that they can bring tears to the eyes of even the mildly discerning. A woman visitor, who had known the place a few years before, was recently heard to exclaim on seeing one of these miscreations 'But surely that is only *temporary!*'

Owing to my continuous residence I am less aware of local changes than if I had been absent for prolonged periods. Changes have taken place although, considering the pressures, the damage, so far, has not been great. Within the last two hundred and fifty years the character of Drumnadrochit was strongly influenced by two very different men. The first was Sir James Grant – the Good Sir James, whom I have already mentioned – and the second was Bradley Martin, an American millionaire. Sir James, who looked after Urquhart from 1761 until he became proprietor in 1773, was an 'improver'; a good and progressive landlord. When he died in 1811 it was said of him that he was 'uniformly guided by rectitude of principle, benevolence of disposition and the most fervent, though rational, piety.'

This Grant was largely responsible for planning and building Milton and Old Lewiston (named after his son, Sir Lewis) as well as his own home village of Grantown-on-Spey. Old Lewiston, by the beginning of the 19th century, had grown to about twenty houses in what is now part of Drumnadrochit. A thatched public house and smithy stood on the site of today's supermarket and houses extended along the line of Balmacaan Road to a school at the west end. By 1803, however, the continuing problem of water supply there, as well as the advantages to the local trade of linen manufacture in housing the workers near a river, led to the creation of the Lewiston we know today on the banks of the Coilty. Gradually the old village fell into decay – by 1808 it was said to resemble 'a mole upon a fine face' while the new houses by the river were 'very neat'.

Bradley Martin, whose unlimited wealth can be gauged by a reference in the *Guinness Book of Records* to a party given by him at the Waldorf Hotel in 1897 costing 369,200 dollars, heard of the Balmacaan Estate and its ponderous mansion in 1881. Three years later he had obtained a full lease from Ian Charles Grant, Earl of Seafield, the great-grandson of James the Good.

Balmacaan House

The Martins lived in colossal style. He took on all the expenses of the estate and the wage bill of its army of workers. He entertained on a lavish scale and married his daughter to an English Earl. Along with the benefits of almost full employment in the Glen, Bradley and his brother Townsend showed many acts of affordable kindness to those in his employ and their dependants. Local children especially loved Townsend who would take them, en masse, to the village shop and buy them sweets. At the end of season, wages were paid in gold sovereigns and the occasion celebrated by a liberal issue of whisky, cheese and biscuits. Of course, like any other successful businessman, Bradley Martin would have had a tough streak in him. F. S. Spencer, his American butler, must have been painfully aware of this when he found himself in insoluble difficulties after having spent household funds entrusted to him on drink and gambling. Smoothing his passage to the next world with whisky, he ostentatiously shot himself on the Balmacaan staircase just before dinner as a huge party was going on. But Bradley Martin was a generous man, and well-liked. He gave the village its village hall and they gave him a fine memorial. When we first came to the Glen, Balmacaan House was in the autumn of its days, a gaunt shell, a dry-rotted, broken-windowed travesty of its erstwhile state. It was demolished in 1972. As the explosive charges rocked the great walls it is said that ghostly faces were seen peering through some upper windows.

Bradley Martin

Another house of similar period but different renown has been treated more leniently by the whims of chance. It is Divach Lodge, a rambling building of wayward elevations and angles, set magnificently above a waterfall and gorge. In the middle 1860s John Phillip R. A. came there to find peace in which to paint. He was followed by his friend Arthur J. Lewis, and others of the worlds of art, literature and the stage. A visitor's book would have contained such names as John Millais and Henry O'Neil, Anthony Trollope and J. M. Barrie, Henry Irving, the Terry Sisters (Kate Terry became Mrs. Arthur Lewis and the grandmother of John and Val Gielgud), the celebrated explorer Robert Falcon Scott, and many others. Later the lodge fell into decay and would have suffered Balmacaan's fate had it not been

Divach Lodge

Over: Telford's Bridge at Invermoriston seen through the arch of its replacement

discovered and lovingly restored by an American woman, and her naturalist friend. Their ministrations have been upheld by the present owners who carry on its tradition by welcoming artist visitors.

Its frenetic seasonal activities apart, Drumnadrochit has the slightly conservative air of a residential village but it is not lacking in worthy projects. For instance, there is the riding school at Borlum Farm which caters for the disabled. And on the high moors north of the village is a fine example of privately financed conservation where conifers are planted in proper numbers on land most fitted to them, native

woodland is honoured for its beauty and left alone, and open moorland is respected for its own wild self. And from that same hill water springs from the ground in a state of such biological perfection that a plan is afoot to bottle and then market it in less fortunate places. It is said that it will be sent even to the States for the greater enjoyment of our whisky there. Daly the Druid, one feels, ought to receive a royalty on every bottle sold; it was he who blessed the water to begin with.

Each Spring we go into a cold sweat in case the tourists do not come but by Autumn we are pleased to see the back of them. For the gregarious and party-minded winters in the Glen are not what they used to be; the freely occurring ceilidh – the spontaneous combustion of fiery spirits when two or three or more were gathered together – is much less common. When we first came here the celebration of the New Year was an outrageous occasion when a whole year's indiscretions could be tirelessly fitted into a few hours, and blamed on the drink. It was usual to travel from house to house, giving and taking whisky, until, in the cold, grey dawn, your legs crumpled under you, and you slept where you dropped. These days such indecorous (but somehow heroic) performances are becoming exceptional.

In the Summer the tourists descend upon Castle Urquhart in their hordes, easily invading the ancient fortress. Now held in trust for the nation by the Scottish Development Department, it is immaculately maintained although the presence of a piper at the parking space and regular visits by a water bus from the New Clansman marina strike a rather incongruous note. But all in all it is a colourful scene on a bright summer's day and not overly disrespectful to those ancient walls. Indeed after all the centuries of strife and plunder they have lived through, it probably provides a welcome change. West of the Castle is the beehive cairn that the local people erected to their hero, John Cobb. It is opposite this point his speedboat *Crusader* disintegrated in 1952 (see p. 136). On the way to Fort Augustus, high above the steel hair nets in which the Roads Department are containing the unruly sandstone, there are devastated slopes dotted with stumps and littered with brash and dead trees. It is not a pretty sight, and there is worse to come; the sapling conifers planted here in 1924 have reached commercial size and are ready for the axe.

Of all the Loch-side villages Invermoriston seems most to have escaped the spoiling touch of change. The hotel, free of incompatible extensions or built-in shops which sell trash to tourists, is just as it was in more gracious pre-war days. The village store opposite is unchanged. The 1930s bridge over the churning River Moriston is very similar in the builders' choice of style and stonework to Telford's 1813 structure a few yards upstream.

Between here and Fort Augustus, a dense thicket separates the road and the water. The huge arch of the Horseshoe Crag across the Loch, once so well seen by motorists, can only be glimpsed nowadays in flashes through the trees. You are almost at Fort Augustus before the Loch is again visible and then the strong outline of the Abbey's clock tower with the village at its feet takes all the attention. In the middle distance is Loch Ness's only island, a low, concave mound, crowned with a symmetry of trees. It is commonly called Cherry Island, a name given to it by Cromwell's people at the Fort, but it is really Eilean Mhuireach, or Murdoch's island. It is a crannog, an ancient artefact, but so striking a part of the modern scene that it calls for inclusion in this chapter. Crannogs are quite commonplace in local lochs (the Hydro Board drowned some of them when loch levels were raised) but this, because of its closeness to a busy shore, is the best known of them. They were designed to provide fortified retreats and were constructed and used between the Iron Age and the 16th century: they remain as testaments to the resource of their builders. This one, which lies about 150 yards from the shore, was investigated in 1908 by Dom Odo Blundell, O. S. B., F. S. A., a monk from the Abbey. Dom Odo was a man who plainly scorned superficial examinations; he put on a diving suit to get to the roots of the matter. There he observed that a raft of oak logs lay on the soft clay of the loch bed. On top of this was a layer of heavy stones which were retained in position by thick posts driven into the deeper gravel. Knowing that Telford's canal work had raised the Loch level by several feet, he concluded that the crannog had once been much larger than its sixty by forty-eight feet; large enough, in fact, to accommodate a small fort, traces of which were still apparent. On the north-west side there were the remains of an underwater causeway. Resting as it does on soft silt the crannog almost justifies the belief of one of Cromwell's troopers that here was an 'island (that) swims in the midst of the ocean' though his further comment that 'it floats from one part of the Lough to the other' plainly infers that eyewitness accounts of Loch Ness phenomena were no more reliable then than they are today.

The Old Military Road (see p. 126)

Loch Ness

Cherry Island,
the Loch's only one

Not long ago I took a walk up the zigzag track that follows the line of the old military road from Fort Augustus to the west. It was a perfect July morning, hot, windless, filled with the rich, dark scents of sweating conifers and the sharper, less cloying birch. As I walked, slowly for my old dog's sake, I thought idly of Johnson and Boswell, and wondered how they would have come to terms with 1987 if they could have glimpsed it from their standpoint in time 214 years before. As a relevant touch to my musings a jet fighter howled across the village and vanished down the race track of Loch Ness. The air rustled behind it and a few dead twigs fell from the fir. I tried to compose a Johnsonian response to this violent affront to the summer calm but my wit was insufficient to the task. Down below me in the village the Abbey clock chimed the hour charmingly, a sound so disconcertingly normal and apt that it, and not the other, made me start. The building that is now the Fort Augustus Monastery and School began to be shaped into its present form in 1876 when the military buildings were gifted to the Order of St Benedict by Lord Lovat. Though the cloister has replaced the cannon there is still something daunting and barrack-like about this trim, solid place with its blunt finger pointing to heaven. Little of Wade's 18th-century fort remains, less, perhaps, than of the earlier Kil-chumin barracks, a wall of which, complete with musket loopholes, can still be seen behind the Lovat Arms Hotel. Within the Abbey are some vaulted brick archways that relate to its military years, but these are about all. More strange is the Roman relief sculpture that depicts three mother-goddesses and dates from the First and Second centuries A.D. How it comes to be here would seem to be a mystery, but it was plainly not brought by the Romans.

J.A. Hansom, architect and cab designer, planned the bulk of the domestic quarters in the last years of his life, around 1880. Peter Paul Pugin, who specialised in churches, was responsible for cloisters, tower and two chapels a decade later. The Romanesque church was only fully completed in 1975. North west of the Abbey, across the canal – these days a water filled artery heavily clotted by cruisers – is the bridge which once carried Cauldfield's 1755 military road across the river Oich. It is dilapidated now, its stones spate-shaken and its timbers rotten, and you cross it at your peril. Up river are the pillars that once supported the ill-fated Invergarry-Fort Augustus railway line on its way to the Pier Station.

Inveroich House, at the top of the narrow strip of land between river and canal, has a long history which includes occupancy by Captain Mark Gwyne who com-manded the Government 'galley' which plied between Lochend (Aldourie) and Fort Augustus after the Fort was completed in 1729. He commanded it, in fact, for fifty years and was almost seventy years in the Navy, having joined as a midship-man at the age of twelve and died, as it were, under sail, at over 80. His own father, who also captained a 'galley', was actually drowned in Loch Ness as he was return-ing on a wild December day from Lochend. The whole family was well respected in

Fort Augustus and in 1827 the Secretary for War petitioned to provide for Mark Gwyne's indigent children. Government pensions were less than generous in those days.

Loch Ness's only true wilderness area is the stretch of shore between Fort Augustus and Foyers. Its only ready land access is from either place or by a path that leads down to a boathouse through the splendid gorge of the River Knockie. Here in unkempt woodland, where trees lie where they have fallen and untrampled moss is thick and green, the Sitka Deer whistle in alarm as you approach; this shore, one feels, is much as it was when man first came upon the earth. If you should walk along it north-east from the Fort you will come across the prominent memorial to Mrs Hambro, a banker's wife, who was tragically drowned when the speedboat in which she was travelling with her husband and son overturned. Below the memorial and amid a jumble of sharply splintered rocks is Corrie's cave. Identified by a great flake which forms one of its sides a serpentine corridor leads to an inner chamber and total darkness. Though I have known it for years I only recently learned the origin of its name. Corrie, or Gorrie, was the familiar name of Alexander Macdonald who was as big a rogue as you would find in a day's march. His speciality was sheep and cattle stealing but he would turn his hand to highway robbery when given half a chance. For years he thumbed his nose at authority but eventually, with every honest man's hand against him, he took up residence in the cave which was already known to him. From this insalubrious but well-hidden retreat he made regular forays, but less audaciously than before. Corrie, it seems, had one redeeming feature – he was a patriot. He had a special spite against the Duke of Cumberland and was determined to assassinate him. With a musket stolen from the Fort he lay in wait for the Hanoverian oppressor and fired at him from behind a rock. But the shot went wide and Corrie fled, hotly pursued by redcoats. He gave them the slip and returned to his cave where he lived for many years until he grew too old to support himself and his wife led him away to die peacefully in the hills behind Fort Augustus.

The modern and recent history of Foyers is bound up with hydro-electricity so I shall leave it for a later chapter. Above the B852 Loch-side road a little west of Inverfarigaig is a pleasant and blandly unobtrusive house called Boleskine, for fourteen years the home of Aleister Crowley, the self-styled 'Great Beast'. It is said that he bought this small estate in 1903 with the object of carrying out some infernal mumbo-jumbo in connection with the invocation of his guardian angel. In his hagiography, *The Legend of Aleister Crowley*, Israel Regardie claims that Crowley was a much maligned man – I am sure he was, and through every fault of his own. He was autocratic, self-adulatory and arrogant, qualities which he took no pains to hide. Almost forgotten when he died in 1947, by then a grey shadow of his black self, he provided enough fuel in the earlier part of the century to fire a best-selling

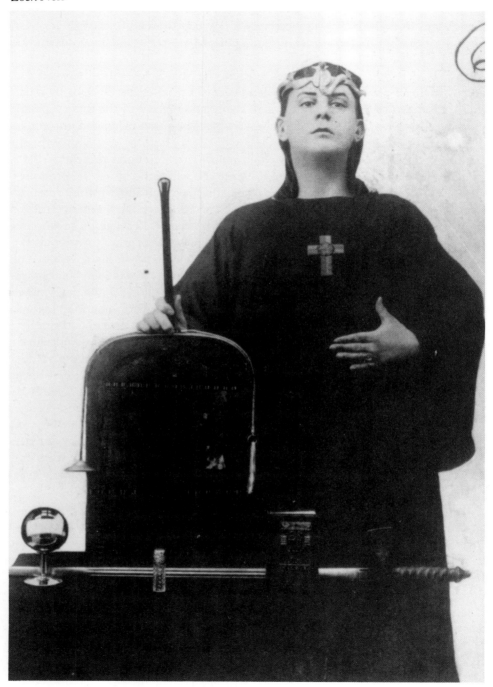

Aleister Crowley

reputation for devilish rites, violent attacks on Christianity and the Establishment and a great variety of mayhem. He was also a poet of controversial merit and a considerable mountaineer.

During his reign at Boleskine rumours flew about the countryside. The Celtic Twilight is an ideal environment for such as he. It is said that he caused a crucifix to be buried beneath the front doormat, a somewhat theatrical device, and there was a circular bed in the house used for I know not what unsavoury purposes. My father used to tell me that tradesmen would not approach the house but preferred to leave Crowley's orders at a safe distance. When he went away from Boleskine he left a trail of occult detritus that was quickly converted into local lore. While there were no hints of such orgies as reputedly took place at the Sicilian abbey at Cefalu, the 'Beast' and his acolytes do seem to have charged the aether at Boleskine with some degree of malevolent force. One highly respected later owner shot himself for no apparent reason, another was involved in a national scandal and some visitors to whom I have spoken protest that they were aware of a poisonous atmosphere in the house.

Although 'ghosts' and 'visitations' are unconcerned with Time or Place one of the hauntings at Boleskine borders on the far-fetched. This is the case of Simon, Lord Lovat's head, legally struck from his body after the '45, which, as I understand it, was wont to roll along the corridors at dead of night. While his lordship is known to have engaged in a skirmish with some men of Athol above Inverfarigaig in 1698 there seems no reason why he should have returned to this area posthumously, especially since the house was not built, albeit by another Fraser of Lovat, until the next century. It may be, of course, that he was waiting in Limbo until he and the Black Magician could get together for a few occult antics.

Moving east towards Dores we can no longer find that testament to General Wade's tenacity, the 1732 blasting of the Black Rock cliff. Sadly, I think, the road here has been recently realigned and the historic and exciting section is replaced by a very dull and ordinary stretch of road. Indeed there is not much of interest nowadays between here and Dores as the shore-line thickets are so dense that little can be seen of the Loch and on the other side blocks of conifers conceal every natural detail of the mountain sides. A much more attractive alternative, though not perhaps for the timid motorist, is to take the road that climbs above the River Farigaig in a series of dramatic zigzags. Though narrow and initially steep, this little road is well surfaced and its bold and uncompromising line is a tribute to its builder, William Fraser-Tytler, and to his father Lord Woodhouselee, a judge of the Court of Session, who financed it in the early 19th century. Once the zigzags are overcome the road provides a superb view of Dun Dearduil. As it drops away behind the little mountain, first seen full face as an expanse of grey slabs and grassy ledges, becomes a tree-clad splinter with the Loch and the long ridge of Mealfuarvonie a perfect

The pe
women
watche
hangin

backcloth. It is one of the classic views of each of these features which encapsulates, for me at any rate, the special flavour of this side of Loch Ness.

Our road, having meandered charmingly through woods and by small farmsteads, joins General Wade's near Loch Ceo Glais. Now we are in high moorland country, built from the sandstone conglomerates, where the hills have round backs and short, deeply lined faces. To the east, across the end of Loch Ceo Glais (pronounced, as written by the Commissioners in 1810, as 'Keglish'), is a low, pointed hill, Tom na Croich; here there was once a gallows on which the Lovat Frasers punished difficult cases. Two old women, with a weakness for such entertainments, used to sit on the opposite bank, just above the road, and watch the hangings. As the years went by their hard hearts became even harder, and eventually each woman was turned completely to stone. They sit there, close together, to this very day, beside the outline of the military road, beneath the hydro-electric lines which modern man has slung so indecorously above their heads.

The B862 road which we have just joined soon plunges steeply down to Dores while a branch, the true line of Wade's original, descends less abruptly to Inverness skirting as it goes Loch Ashie, one of the two lochs which supply the town with water. Dores has grown gracefully around its inn. On this site there was a 'King's house' in Hanoverian times, a drinking place for the soldier builders of the military road. Such places often sprang up near roadside construction camps. The present Dores Inn is smart but unspoilt, a pleasant place to call on a summer's evening when the Loch, almost at its back door, is calm and serene.

If you turn right at the top of the hill on the Inverness road and take a minor road that leads back to Ashie Moor you will soon come across a pair of gates and a turnstyle which open into a wild garden. Little notices, phrased in McGonagall-style rhyme, ask the public not to steal the plants. Climbing a slope, on which white heather abounds beneath the birch, by either of two paths you will find an engraved slab set in a wall and guarded by two magnificent bronze wildcats; here your curiosity about the place will be satisfied. This, as the legend tells you, is Kinchyle, and the garden is 'dedicated to the memory of Clan Macbean of long ago whose ancient chiefs once owned extensive lands in this area'. The garden was established as recently as 1961 by the present chief of the Clan. Although, as a poem points out, there are no bodies buried here this modern place, set in a pristine land, offers a sense of that ultimate comfort and security that one sometimes feels, when the mood is right, in isolated country churchyards.

It is a fitting place to end one's journey round the Loch.

8 Speedboats, a Bomber and Submarines

ON THE 29th August 1952 the jet-engined powerboat *Crusader* was unloaded from a lorry at Temple Pier, near Drumnadrochit. Not surprisingly it caused immense local interest. By then most Loch-siders and visitors must have read or heard that the 52-year-old London fur broker, John Cobb – who already held the land speed record at over 390 miles an hour – was going for a double first, and Loch Ness had been chosen because of its singular length and straightness and because it was much less crowded than other British lakes. Its only obvious drawback was that it lies in the line of the prevailing south-west wind.

As in an attempt on a Himalayan peak, the timing was important. There the best moment was just before the monsoon and here it was at the tail end of summer before the autumn equinox. The boat had to be delivered, tested, tried and ready, all within the space of a very few weeks. Ever since Sir Frank Whittle had pioneered it eleven years earlier the development and application of the jet engine had been a stimulating challenge to engineers. In the latter days of the war the Gloster Meteor, powered by twin turbo jets, joined the veteren Spitfire in outstripping and destroying Hitler's flying bombs, to the great relief of the inhabitants of south-east England. By 1952 air speeds achieved by jet propulsion had edged up to that point where an aircraft would collide with its own sound with little understood results. It was becoming clear, however, that such velocity produced a punishing turbulence on the wings and fusilage. It would do so on water too. It would need to be flat calm if speeds in excess of 200 mph were to be achieved without unacceptable hazard. Waves travel before the wind but in deep water their substance hardly moves at all.

Under compression water becomes as unyielding as steel; anyone who has made a belly flop from a five-metre diving board can tell you that, as can the driver of a powerboat travelling at as little as 15 knots in choppy water. A completely windless day was essential to success.

The full-throated howl of the jet engine – so familiar nowadays to Lochness-siders – was first heard two days after *Crusader*'s arrival there. Firmly fastened to the pier by steel ropes to hold her still her Ghost jet engine was run up to testing power. This powerful unit, the same as was fitted in the *Comet* airliner, was designed to consume 60–80 tons of air per minute and the effects of its superheated jet stream can still be found on a local tree. The noise was deafening, causing those in attendance to cover their ears while the echoes roared back from the surrounding hills.

By the 5th September John Cobb had worked *Crusader* up to 140 mph on the Loch and was said to be quietly confident. Yet, bold and fearless as he was, the next day's news of John Derry's death when his De Havilland 110 jet fighter broke up as it touched the sound barrier at the Farnborough Air Show must have been sobering.

John Cobb

For the next two days the wind gusted on the Loch, preventing, at the last moment, a high-speed trial run on the 10th. The strain upon all concerned in the project – especially the man who was to sit in the cockpit – can only be imagined. But the air currents around Loch Ness are capricious and by the morning of the 11th, an astonishing change had taken place. The black surface was mirror calm. Cobb took his boat into position opposite Urquhart Castle for a fast run. He had no sooner started than a fresh problem arose. The immense thrust failed to get her up onto her sponsons – the floats designed to lift her into the planing position – because the water was too *calm*. A slight corrugation of the surface was needed to get her up to the critical angle. This was obtained by motoring a dinghy across her course, but structural modifications were plainly required. *Crusader*'s leviathan-like struggles created a complex wave pattern that was inevitably taken (then as now, and in the future) as further evidence of an unknown creature. It showed, moreover, that it was neither shy of company nor upset by noise.

sader
ges beside
Loch

135

The team now took *Crusader* out of the water to work on her. A diesel-electric mobile crane was used to lift the 3 ton 31 foot boat. Five days later Cobb was satisfied and sent for timekeepers of the Motor Marine Association, but made it clear to the Press that no attempt on the record would be made until conditions were perfect. It then stood at 178.4 mph, an average of the outward and return sprint over the measured mile, established by Stanley Sayres in 1952.

By now, on Loch Ness, local and national interest had reached fever pitch. Human beings, especially those who live humdrum lives, seem to have a compulsive and morbid need to experience extreme danger at no risk to themselves, and so on Friday 19th some seven thousand vultures were in position around the Lochside. A bus had left Inverness at 5.30 a.m. bound for the arena. Spectators came from as far north as Wick, as far south as Glasgow and Edinburgh, and beyond. John Cobb did not disappoint his huge audience. After an uncertain start *Crusader* tore into the measured mile and covered it in 20 seconds flat: 180 mph. Cobb's hopes must have been high but the return run was spoiled by increasing side winds and his mean average for both runs was 173.14 mph. It was a pointer to what might be done when conditions were perfect.

They were far from perfect over the next seven days. They included the Autumnal Equinox on the 23rd, a point in the year which is often characterised by heavy rain and strong winds. Indeed the Highlands now seemed to be suffering a replica of the torrential downpour that had devasted Lynmouth in Devon a month earlier. The rivers that feed Loch Ness were swollen with flood water and brown with peat, carrying dead branches and even tree trunks in their spate.

One cannot help wondering what pressures persuaded John Cobb to snatch at victory on the 29th when, for a brief moment, the deteriorating weather stayed its hand. An official attempt was scheduled for early that morning but at 8.55 a.m. it was cancelled as a light south-east wind teased the surface into two-inch ripples. By 9.35 a.m. it had grown worse. Then just as quickly it improved and soon it was dead calm at Foyers at the west end of the course. *Crusader*, lifted out of the water for examination at Temple Pier, was quickly returned to it, and it was obvious to the innumerable spectators that events were marching towards their climax. The timekeepers' motor boats took up their positions, leaving arrow-shaped creases on the glassy surface.

Just before noon Cobb came round to the starting point and ran up his engines to full power. *Crusader* rose up on her sponsons like a bird and roared away, leaving a trail of white foam behind her. No one had ever seen her travel so fast. Those who remember say that she hardly touched the water, and she was moving at over 200 mph when she came out of the measured mile. Then the decelerating powerboat bounced twice and recovered for a split second before breaking up in a flurry of spray and debris. John Cobb was killed instantly although a cruelly mistaken

report by the BBC told that he had escaped with minor injuries. Seldom has the line between triumph and disaster been so thin. Cheers and groans were combined in single cries and as the raucous echoes died away people returned to their cars or homes and their humdrum lives. Another Roman Holiday was over.

The post mortem was necessarily inconclusive. Some blamed an iron-hard ripple, others suggested a floating log. It may have been that John Cobb decelerated too quickly, subjecting the hull to unimaginable strain. Water may have entered the turbines and caused them to explode. A definitive explanation might have saved Donald Campbell fifteen years later on Coniston Water when he and his *Bluebird* went the same tragic way at 328 mph. Some will always say, what a waste of good men. And it is true that such as Cobb and Campbell are examples of a special breed, the natural leaders, the aspirants to high adventure who will go 'always a little futher'.

What else should such men do?

Surviving fragments of Crusader *are burnt*

137

In wartime there is work enough for them, and to spare. Flight Lieutenant J. B. Stewart was one of the bold pilots who flew with 149 Squadron on the first British raid on Heligoland. He attacked a merchantman with unconfirmed results. It was the 3rd December 1939 and Stewart's aircraft was a Wellington bomber with some recent modification. With a wing span of 86 feet and a length of 64 feet its empty weight was just over 8 tons, and it could fly at a top speed of 235 mph. It was a MK IA, its number was N2980, and its squadron letter was R for Robert.

The Wellingtons, in these early days, paid a terrible price for idiocy in high places, an ingrained pre-war belief that the bomber would always get through. R for Robert was a lucky aircraft, completing fourteen missions in around nine months at a time when the life expectancy of the breed was little more than six. In October of 1940 N2980 was sent for a respite to No. 20 O.T.U. Lossiemouth.

Now we come to the fateful New Year's Eve of 1940. At 3 p.m. R for Robert lifted off the runway at Lossiemouth on a navigational training flight across the north of Scotland. Its course was to take it along part of the Great Glen, to the Island of Canna and back to its base after passing over Golspie. It was a cold day with frequent snow showers even at lower levels. It is easy to imagine that the pilot, Squadron Leader Marwood-Elton, his co-pilot P/O Slatter and his crew of six trainee navigators had been looking forward to a New Year party at the station, most probably their first in Scotland. If all had gone well they would have been in plenty of time for it; R for Robert could have completed her flight in less than two hours. But all did not go well. Flying at a height of around 8000 feet, they ran into a snowstorm over the Monadhliath hills, south of Loch Ness. I have some reason to remember that wintry evening as I myself, on much less important business, was in those same hills with two friends. Following a whim we had planned to see the New Year in from the top of a mountain above the village of Daviot; at around 3 p.m. we were probably drinking tea in a derelict farmhouse which we sometimes used as a base. It is likely that R for Robert would have passed overhead.

The Wellington's starboard engine failed when they were somewhere over Foyers. Marwood-Elton knew that he had an emergency on his hands; in such conditions he could not maintain height on a single engine. He ordered the six trainees to bail out. Most tragically – and ironically as matters were to turn out – Sgt. Fensome, the rear gunner, was killed when his parachute failed to open. The others landed safely in various places. Marwood-Elton and Slatter were now very much on their own with their struggling aircraft rushing on through clouds of grey murk. At that time of year it is already dusk in the Scottish highlands.

One can imagine their intense relief when they saw, through a break in the storm cloud, the long stretch of black water which they recognised as Loch Ness. Here was a God-sent chance to ditch the Wellington. The squadron leader banked R for Robert so that they began to descend in a north-easterly direction parallel to and not far from the A 82 road. I have no knowledge of flying, except as a passenger, but I should think that to set down a big aircraft with a dead engine in near darkness on an unfamiliar loch requires enormous skill and judgement. Marwood-Elton did it perfectly. Then, with unhurried confidence, he and P/O Slatter climbed out onto a wing, detached their dinghy and paddled to the shore. Before they reached it R for Robert had sunk out of sight. The pilot thought sadly this was the last that any-body would ever see of her. A lorry driver, bound for Inverness, must have been amazed at the sight of two airmen in full flying kit standing by the roadside. He stopped and gave them a lift.

In the crofts above Lochend, a mile or so to the east, folk were lighting their oil lamps and preparing to drink in the New Year. Only one of them, Jimmy Cameron, is remembered as having seen the plane come down. To the east my small party had set out to climb our mountain. It was to be a strange night with the frosty darkness punctuated by flashes of St Elmo's Fire. As we went I am sure we must have spared a thought for an older companion who had already joined the R.A.F. As was the fashion of those times he had grown up quickly, putting aside childish things with indecent haste. He was sixteen when we climbed together above Loch Ness: he, too, was flying a Wellington when he 'bought it' three years later and was buried in Holland.

R for Robert lay in a cushion of silt beneath two hundred feet of water for the next thirty-six years. Few residents and fewer passers-by even knew that it was there. In fact it took a mounting interest in something quite different to establish its exact position. Engaged in a vastly optimistic search for the bones of the plesiosaur (or its modern descendants) an American team, Klein Associates Inc., recorded the outline of an aircraft (along with some prehistoric stone circles – see p. 113) in 1976, using sonar. National pride, one supposes, led to the immediate suggestion that it was one of theirs – a PBY Catalina flying boat. From the excellent sonar trace it certainly does not look like one. The Catalina had blunt wing tips and no tail turret. In the trace the right-hand wing is plainly pointed (one senses that the left hand one is partly buried in silt) and the outline of the turret can be strongly infer-red. I fancy that a keen plane spotter of the war years might have guessed right first time. But this is really no matter. In June 1977 the American research team gave a lecture in Inverness to describe what they had found. Two members of the Heriot-Watt University's Underwater Technology Group, present at the lecture, saw a chance for practical tests on a remotely-operated underwater television system and resolved to photograph the aircraft at close quarters. The next summer they did so, confirming that it was indeed R for Robert and in excellent condition considering its prolonged immersion. Part of the canvas was stripped from the wings and fusi-lage, clearly revealing the geodetic construction that Barnes Wallis (the designer also of the 'bouncing' and other bombs) had first used in the frame of the R 100

airship, before applying it to the bomber.

The Underwater Technology Group returned to Loch Ness in 1980 to pursue research, carry out practical tests on underwater acoustic navigation systems, and to experiment with the idea of an unmanned tetherless submersible. But like Everest, R for Robert was still there and its recovery was a continuing challenge. In that year the Group put forward an ambitious plan to use ANGUS 003 (in full, A Navigable General-Purpose Underwater Surveyor) which had sent up the pictures of the aircraft two years earlier, to attach lifting gear to it by remote control. This, if it could be done, would be a triumph of underwater technology. Money was now the problem. But by 1981 they had sufficient funds to take a second look and what they saw came as a considerable shock. Vandals had been at work! No one had claimed responsibility – as they say in terrorist incidents – but the damage was sufficiently massive to weaken the structure. It would now require the services of a professional deep-diving company to bring the Wellington to the surface intact.

By 1984, after further examination, it was clear that 'unknown human agency' was going to accomplish what fourteen missions over Germany, a ditch landing and forty-four years in two hundred feet of water had not – the final destruction of R for Robert. The only way to halt this distinctly tasteless trophy hunting was to get the aircraft out of harm's way and, to this end, The Loch Ness Wellington Association Ltd. was formed in 1984. In the lavishly produced booklet "The Story of 'Another' Loch Ness Monster" Group Captain Paul Harris, D.F.C., R.A.F. (Retd) described its aims. These were to lift the aircraft and donate it to the Brooklands Museum of motor-racing and aviation which was to be opened in Weybridge in 1987. It was at Weybridge that Sir Barnes Wallis designed its geodetic structure and there it was built by Vickers-Armstrong in 1939. It was a splendidly appropriate idea that R for Robert should at last come home, especially since of the 11,461 Wellingtons produced, only one other then remained. To complete this sense of home and family who could be better suited to head the Association than Paul Harris who, flying a Wellington, had been the first man to lead a bombing raid on Germany in the Second World War.

The Association was soon in touch with a number of companies who were helpful in offering materials, expertise and manpower in support of the project. A special lifting frame was designed to take the weight of the aircraft evenly and thus prevent destructive stresses. To fix the cables and lifting bags to the wings and fuselage divers were to use the WASP, an atmospheric diving suit for use at great depths. The whole complex operation was scheduled to take place in September 1985, and was as much dependent on calm weather as had been John Cobb's record breaking attempt in *Crusader* thirty-three years earlier. September can be as gentle as a kitten or as savage as a bull; that year it was bullish. When a brief moment of calm came it had to be snatched. By now public interest was aroused and the usual

Left: the raising of R for Robert. A wing emerges from the Loch.

Over: the front of the Wellington about to be put on a barge

gawping masses were in attendance. Three miles of the A 82, from Brackla to Dochfour, were narrowed by parked cars and the beach from Lochend to Bona was thick with curious onlookers.

The long awaited lift began on the night of 17th September. The aluminium frame hung above the aircraft and the uninflated lifting bags were strapped to the more solid parts of the wings and fusilage. The dark surface of the Loch was untroubled, a factor essential to success as a swell would have produced a destructive snatching action far below. Gradually air was pumped into the bags and very gently the cables took the strain. On the bed of the Loch the aircraft shivered and stirred, like a cold giant wakening from sleep.

In a magical few moments cautious optimism was replaced by mounting jubilation. Men held their breaths, too intent even to cheer, as it became clear that R for Robert was two metres off the bottom and still coming up. Then – well, we have hanging in a lavatory here a poster which depicts the official opening of a Victorian railway bridge. A locomotive has triumphantly steamed onto a span which has suddenly collapsed beneath its weight. The welcoming committee stand aghast. Somebody, most probably the chairman, says 'O, shit!' Such bleak understatement would have been on the lips of all those who saw the cables heave and twitch as R for Robert fell back into the silt. Eight tons of Wellington and heaven only knows how much muddy suction had buckled the lifting frame. And that was not all. The fusilage, already fatally weakened by the vandals' mindless work, had been broken in two in a tug of war between the restraining silt and the lifting gear.

It must have been a sombre moment for the recovery team. R for Robert, for whose immaculate restoration so many plans had been made, was now much more of a ruin than it had been when first located in 1976. It might have lain complete in the Loch bed until in the fullness of geological time it became a fossil, a source of interest to galactic visitors. It was obviously incumbent on those most concerned to finish this flawed operation, but it was not going to be easy. The lifting frame, a complex structure fashioned in aluminium by the Vintage Aircraft and Flying Association, had been made in Weybridge; time and distance alone precluded any replacement from that source. Instead Cromarty Firth Engineering took on the job of constructing a tough, simple steel frame capable of carrying up the sections one by one. They completed it in double quick time and it was ready for its vital role in a further lifting attempt only three days later.

At this point I should like to quote Robin Holmes, a leading member of the Underwater Technology Group, 'At 10.30 on the night of the 20th September, 1985, the compressed air was turned on to the first set of submerged buoyancy bags. Each of the seven stages was completed in roughly forty-five minutes. The last set of buoyancy bags appeared on the surface at 2.00 a.m. on Saturday 21st September, completing a lift of sixty-five metres. I have been told by an authority in marine salvage that the Wellington recovery is the deepest known salvage by air bags.' I am glad that he allowed himself this little flash of triumph; the rest of his account is over-modest. Alfie Lyden of Oceaneering Ltd was the man in overall charge of the operation with John Wise of J. W. Automarine Ltd as the air bag specialist, but it was Holmes who had nurtured the seed of the idea for seven difficult years until it reached fruition. There was well-deserved and round-the-clock roistering at the Clansman Hotel at Brackla, the headquarters of the operation.

Once on the surface the wings and forward fuselage were towed to the canal and river entrance at Bona and lifted onto a barge in front of an enormous audience. The following day the tail plane and gun turret were recovered. After the sections were dismantled their component parts were transported by barge down Telford's canal to Muirtown at Inverness, and thence by road to Weybridge. Only the front turret, which had broken off during the recovery operation, was left behind. A deterioration in the weather along with other factors made it impossible to bring it up then. But it was by no means forgotten. The Loch Ness Wellington Association mounted a final expedition in the Spring of 1987 which included a Royal Navy Fleet Diving Group, Heriot-Watt University, Ametek Offshore (Scotland) Ltd., U.D.I. Group Ltd., and Caley Cruisers Ltd. Ametek provided a ROV (a remotely

The Wellington's gun turret safely caught

operated vehicle under cable control) to examine the turret for its general condition and the best lifting points. On 13th May the team managed to attach a line to a single bolt and began to feed in their monstrous fish with an angler's skill and caution. When it broke surface they even used a landing net to ensure that it did not escape them! Robin Holmes describes the operation as very 'dicey', a word most apt for its wartime R.A.F. connotations, and tells me that it 'succeeded on the last day by good fortune'. With its twin Browning machine guns still jutting aggressively, the turret was soon on its way to Weybridge to join R for Robert in full restoration. There the aircraft will be on display when the museum opens this year.

The Loch Ness Wellington Association, who bore all the costs of the final lift, intends to place a memorial stone opposite the point where the aircraft lay for so many years.

In the summer of 1969 another product of Vickers engineering – they had built the Wellington – entered Loch Ness at Temple Pier. This was *Pisces*, a two man submersible, which had been sent to Loch Ness for its freshwater trials. *Pisces* was a chunky, compact machine, displacing eleven tons, powered by two electric motors capable of driving it along under water at around four knots. It appeared to work very well and by the end of June it had achieved a depth of 400 feet. Later, on the 8th July, it did even better by sitting on the bottom at 820 feet, which appeared to upset the long-held notion that Loch Ness's deepest point was only 754 feet. On their subaqueous wanderings the crew saw a good few fish and some large and very wan looking eels, but apart from these there was nothing to write home about.

But above water some very odd things were happening. Urquhart Castle was being ringed with scaffolding, in Glenurquhart a large private house suddenly sprouted a sign which read Station Hotel and, most wonderful of all, at Temple Pier a plastic-coated frame was rapidly assuming the form of a prehistoric monster. These weird manifestations were the work of Mirisch Films Ltd, who had come to Loch Ness to make sequences for their film, *The Private Life of Sherlock Holmes*. It must be said at once that Sir Arthur Conan Doyle probably turned in his grave when this shocking but witty parody of his work was eventually released.

Mirisch had arranged with the owners of *Pisces* that when the submersible's trials were over they would hire it with the object of towing their mock-up plesiosaur. Onlookers unfamiliar with the ways of film production companies must have thought that the expense of the hire along with the £5000 which the 'monster' cost to build meant it was to be the star of the show. In the event it appeared on the screen for less than a minute. But Mirisch was not short of money. It spent a lot in the Glen, in one way or another. It came to my ears that the film company was looking for small boats to carry 'mist making' machines which would add some atmosphere to the 'monster' sequence. Since I had a boat on the Loch and some

146

spare time I volunteered my services. They were booked for ten days at what I thought was a generous remuneration.

Sadly my boat – a fourteen-foot former sailing dinghy called *Curlew* – had not long been returned to the water, and had partially dried out. Its lower planks were tight and it was a dry boat with one man in it, but with extra weight it leaked fearfully through the upper, shrunken planks. I half guessed that this might happen but dishonestly kept quiet about it in the hope that the 'mist making' machine would not greatly increase *Curlew's* displacement. My hopes were dashed on the first morning when two large men waded into the water with a thing that resembled a small car engine. After much grunting the three of us got it into the *Curlew* near its stern. The boat was now fast in the shingle and it required a concentrated effort to free it. In the process one man's boots filled with water and he cursed unhappily. I prayed, fearing that much worse things were about to befall him.

Under different circumstances it would have been a delightful day for boating. There was a hot sun overhead and Urquhart Bay was sheltered from the brisk east wind that ruffled the water further out. Two other boats were already making smoke and very soon *Curlew* started to do the same. Some water was coming in but much less than I had feared and my baling was equal to its task. It was only when we got into rough water near the Castle that things began to get hectic. It was clear that *Curlew* was on the point of sinking and would not get back to Temple Pier unless she was rid of some of the weight. My two companions seemed to be lost in a kind of theatrical detachment from which even my cry of 'Overboard with the Cargo' or 'Abandon Ship' would not have awakened them. I noticed that we were now making steam instead of smoke. Luckily the shore beside the Castle was within a couple of hundred yards so I opened the throttle of the Seagull outboard to maximum and motored furiously towards it.

We crunched on the shingle with about six inches of freeboard, a waterlogged 'mist maker' and two very wet men who said 'Cheers' with extraordinary unconcern, and went off to the Mirisch canteen for lunch. They told me that they would get some mates to give a hand with the machine. Later, when this had been man-handled up the shore, I left *Curlew* fully immersed so that her planks might tighten. By the next morning she was much more lochworthy and I took her back across the bay to await a further call on my services. Not greatly to my surprise none came. I lingered patiently for eight more days but nobody gave me a glance. Instructions were hard to get as the people in charge were as elusive as the creature out in the Loch. One day as I was hanging about near the pier I noticed some chaps gathered round a large glass tank in which some paper was smouldering. Soon after, a film camera was brought and the Loch was photographed through the rising smoke. It was obvious from their pleased smiles that a simple way of providing mist effects had been found. On the tenth day I applied with some diffidence for my one day's hire money. After *Curlew's* unsatisfactory if not dangerous performance I didn't really expect that it was due. But the pay clerk was adamant. 'That's your money', he said, 'Sign here', and he gave me a huge wad of notes. They covered the whole ten days' hire.

Loch-side residents were just getting used to the sight of a fantasy made flesh when the Mirisch mock-up monster was taken from them. On July 22nd it developed a leak in a buoyancy tank and sank just east of Urquhart Bay in 600 feet of water. The crew of *Pisces* made a determined effort to locate it but, as far as I know, it was never seen again. Some say that the true beast was so irritated by the way its shape was being taken in vain that it sank the model with a single blow from a flipper.

During that silly season summer *Pisces* was not the only submersible in the Loch.

Viper Fish *submerged with its harpoon contraption clearly visible.*

An earnest and stubborn young American had brought his very midget *Viper Fish* at the request of the Loch Ness Investigation Bureau. At once nicknamed 'The Yellow Submarine', Dan Taylor's two-ton toy was fitted with miniature harpoons designed to enter reptilian hide and extract a sample of flesh. The problem was, of course, to get within fifteen feet of the target, this being the harpoons' range. *Viper Fish* was neither a practical idea nor a great success here. To start with it sprang leaks and was at all times unmanageable and slow: local people feared for the life of the bold young submariner who on one occasion reached a depth of 180 feet in Urquhart Bay. With their tiny range no one believed that his harpoons could harm their objective. In London, however, they were less certain about the beast's safety. On the 18th July the House of Lords debated the matter, and doubts were cast upon the propriety of 'potting it with airgun pellets'. Lord Lovat summed up the situation neatly when he hailed the subject in question as one of our most important invisible assets. Dan Taylor, despite his vessel's ineffectual performance, deserves to be remembered as one of the Loch's great explorers. Alone in his tiny capsule he had reached silty bottom in his blind search for this williest-of-wisps. It must have taken

Dan Taylor in his yellow submarine Viper Fish.

a lot of nerve, this solitary adventuring. Taylor differed from Wing Commander Ken Wallis only in his choice of elements; nearly a decade earlier the latter, also at the request of the L.N.I.B., had buzzed across the surface of the Loch in his home-made autogyro, not much bigger than a dragonfly.

The latest great happening on the Loch opened in 1987 with a deafening fanfare from the media. It was the most widely advertised and the least impressive (from anybody's point of view) of all the Loch Ness spectaculars. On Friday October 9th, a pleasant Autumn day, I drove the few miles east from Drumnadrochit to watch the opening of Operation Deepscan. In the car park of the New Clansman Hotel, the local headquarters of the operation, specialist and other vehicles were wedged nose to bumper and every layby towards Inverness was filled. From the narrow shore below I had my first clear view of a string of fussy little cruisers, with their attendant command vessel and pair of circling speedboats, chugging south-westward in line of battle. These boats were crewed by young people from the Docklands Trust and the Drake Fellowship. Overflown by a helicopter, it all looked rather like an updated parody of the Dunkirk evacuation.

Interested as always in the public's reaction to unusual spectacles, I assumed the guise of an anonymous tourist and enquired innocently what was afoot. The man to whom I spoke told me that he had heard a huge net was suspended beneath the cruisers' keels. 'They are trying to drive IT in front of them', he said seriously. 'Reckon they'll have a job'. I agreed that it would be a monster task and wondered how, in view of all the media publicity, he could remain so unenlightened, before remembering that people on holiday often make a point of never listening to the news. Yet he was right enough about the 'net', only it was not a physical one. This was a sonar screen, drawn half way across the Loch, and woven by the impulses of some two score sets of an advanced kind of side-scan computer graph recorder, provided by Lowrance Electronics of Tulsa, Oklahoma, U.S.A.

Operation Deepscan was the original brainchild of cryptozoologist Adrian Shine, in my opinion as honest a man as ever gazed into these waters. It was lavishly, but not disinterestedly, sponsored by the proprietors of the Official Monster Exhibition at Drumnadrochit, Mr James Hogan of Caley Cruisers (who supplied the boats), the Highland Development Board, and others. Since there is only one kind of publicity everybody stood to make more money in the long run whatever the scientific findings, or even the lack of them. The extent of media interest in this show can be judged by the fact that some 250 newspersons and over 20 T.V. crews from various countries (you name them, they were there) had descended upon our Loch; they came, I think hardly fortuitously, at that time of year when the tourist season is normally in decline. The best prizes, as always, went to the strong and ready.

On that Friday the first sweep ended at Fort Augustus, and there followed an amiable 'debriefing' at the New Clansman. Adrian Shine, to whom many of the Press were looking for newsworthy tidings, reported the day's results in his careful undramatic fashion; three large mid-water contacts had been made and Darrell Lowrance, another cautious man as far as mysteries were concerned, went so far as to say that one of these was stronger than any he had seen from such a depth. This was sober but not unhopeful news and, as one would expect in a good hostelry, a mood of inspirited euphoria soon prevailed.

The next day, Saturday, dawned wet but improved later. The boats nosed back from Fort Augustus, gathering a few interesting tracings on their graphs as they came. At headquarters the germ of some rumour had been somehow implanted and there was mounting excitement as the evening's 'debriefing' began. It was heightened by the fact that the T.V. monitors were coyly covered up like Christmas presents awaiting the moment of celebration. When the information came it fell below expectations before taking an unexpected twist. Shine, having shown some nice pictures of fish shoals at varying depths – not at all what was wanted – became devil's advocate when he revealed that some work had been going on that had, in his opinion, demolished an old idol. The location in Urquhart Bay of famous American photographs of the Monster – the 'gargoyle head' and the 'bagpipes in a snowstorm' – had been investigated by a diver. What he found there was a rotting tree stump, the probable origin of gargoyle and bagpipes. This pained the Press and promoted contention between the supporters of rival hypotheses.

Shine's dismissive use of the term 'media monster' (in other words, a plesiosaur)

Operation Deepscan: the fleet of cabin cruisers receives its briefing.

contained a hint of scientific snobbery and did nothing to cheer up the party, and the next day many of the disillusioned reporters went home. Operation Deepscan had kept Loch Ness in the public eye but had done little to solve its mystery. It left a few unexplained sonar contacts but one cannot believe that their examination will justify another expedition on this scale. It seems strange to me, as a layman, why such a penetrating survey – Lowrance's equipment is said to be able to separate fish only four inches apart – failed to locate or identify such obvious artefacts as the head and neck of the Mirisch monster or Cobb's jet engine. It is possible, of course, that these objects are buried deeply in the silt.

The legend will remain; the man who stands in a busy street and points excitedly to the sky will always attract a crowd. And what a let-down it is for all when he is found to be a joker beneath an empty sky! Mr Naohiro Nakamura, of Japanese television, is said to have replied to a reporter's question about his belief in the invisible star of the show: 'All people like to believe in legends. It's an interesting and harmless story, don't you think?'

9 Power and Industry on the Loch

FEW PEOPLE who drive along Loch Ness-side on the A 82 road can fail to notice, some with shocked surprise, the huge, squat building low down on the opposite shore; many wonder what it is, and what purpose it can possibly serve. This egregious object is the Hydro-Electric Board's pumped storage station at Foyers. It is a pity it is so ill-favoured, and one wonders why its designers should have chosen to paint it white, a colour which hugely emphasises its sheer size and angular lines. Decorated in dark green or brown, it would have harmonised much better with the tree-clad slope behind it. But having complained about its looks one must immediately applaud it for the way it performs a necessary function with the utmost morality. In common with all devices that harness water and gravity to make electricity, it is clean, quiet, harmless and still highly productive. No one who lives near this gentle giant need fear far-reaching explosion or slow sickening of its workers and their children, and it adds less poison to the atmosphere than does a single coal-burning cottage fire. It must be said, however, that its pumping function, which I shall describe, is dependent on the continuous operation of the Board's nuclear stations.

Fort Augustus on Loch Ness has an early history of hydro-electric power. In 1890 some mechanically minded monks at the Benedictine Abbey built a small water turbine which supplied the Abbey and part of the village with electric light. Housed in a tiny building and operating under a 'head' of less than fifty feet, the generator made sufficient electricity to light the equivalent of a hundred and eighty 100 watt bulbs. An ingenious touch was provided by a rake, driven by a paddle wheel, which kept the water intake free of leaves and debris. This water turbine and its generator went on working through two world wars and was finally put to rest when the Hydro-Electric Board took over in 1951.

Foyers pumped storage power station

The topography and geological formation of the Foyers area was naturally suited to the establishment of a hydro-electric plant, and this fact was recognised by the British Aluminium Company when they chose to site their factory there in 1895. The conversion of bauxite (which would be carried to the factory through the Caledonian Canal) into aluminum needs a very powerful electric current – some nine units to every pound of the product – so a great and continuous force of water was necessary at the turbines. The twin lochs of Garth and Farraline in Stratherrick were two miles distant and some six hundred feet higher than the delta at Foyers on which the factory was to stand. The catchment of these two lochs which then drained freely into the River Foyers was considerable and the annual rainfall of fifty-eight inches ensured continuity of water flow.

155

Loch Ness

The British Aluminium Company had the best man in the business to advise them. Lord Kelvin, two years old when the Caledonian Canal was first opened, was in his late 70s when he became electrical consultant to the scheme. Its bold execution and successful operation owed much to the mature wisdom and innovative genius of a man who had seen the hydro-electric potential of Niagara Falls. There is an early photograph of him with Lady Kelvin and others at Foyers. With his magnificent white beard and top hat he looks like a Moses who has just struck the rock.

The old British Aluminium Company power station at Foyers

The work of building this great industrial complex fell into three parts. First there was the drilling of two miles of tunnel through the capricious granites and breccias of the hills between the upper lochs and Loch Ness. Then the factory had to be built and furnished with its nine turbines and smelting machinery. Finally earth embankment dams were constructed at the south-west end of Loch Garth to cause that loch to combine with Loch Farraline and form the reservoir, henceforward to be known as Loch Mhor. It is a little unfortunate that this development placed a restriction on the River Foyers and spoilt, except in times of flood, the performance of the famous falls.

I cannot find an account of the building of the British Aluminium Company's works on Loch Ness but *The Children of the Dead End*, a semi-fictional tale of 'hard men' at Kinlochleven during the similar construction work there, probably provides a recognisable picture of Foyers. The men were a tough, hard-drinking crew who were certainly not afraid of a day's work. To have burrowed through miles of friable granite with tools that appear primitive today proves that beyond any doubt. One can only imagine the excitement that followed the meeting of the opposing tunnellers in the bowels of the earth.

By the end of the 19th century Foyers, once known mainly for its Falls, had become a hive of industry. In 1904 the smelter was producing one thousand tons of aluminium annually and this output was to continue, in greater or lesser measure, for the next sixty-three years. In each of the two world wars production was stepped up and then over five hundred men were employed, a fact which accounts for the terraced houses built by the Company to accommodate the workers and their families. But it does not need an army to run the present Pumped Storage station and today many of these houses are empty while others are let as holiday cottages.

The contribution of the Foyers smelter to wartime industry did not escape the Luftwaffe who sent a single Heinkel III there on the 13th February 1941, just weeks after our Wellington had ditched in the Loch. The big machine flew low over the undefended factory and dropped two 500 lb. bombs on it. The results in terms of damage were poor, and it is tragic that a man should have been killed. Despite the vulnerabilty of the target one bomb missed it altogether while the other struck the coping stone of the factory and exploded on the hillside, fracturing some pipes. By the next day the factory had returned to partial production and within a short time all was back to normal.

Eyewitnesses remember that the German pilot circled low over the delta and waved nonchalantly to school children in the playground. Then he flew north, crossing the Loch with apparent unconcern. But he had, in fact, been spotted as he approached Foyers by an officer of the Observer Corps which maintained a post at Bunloit south-west of Castle Urquhart and as he flew over this post on his way home he came under fire from the occupant's Mannlicher rifle. This was ineffective but the observer had already alerted the R. A. F. station at Evanton on the Cromarty Firth and a fighter was airborne and ready. The Heinkel was brought down.

The British Aluminium Company gave up the smelting operation at Foyers in 1967 as the plant was no longer large enough or its position sufficiently economic when compared with deep seawater harbours, to keep it viable. The Hydro-Electric Board, then in its nineteenth year of existence, took over. After having obtained approval for the Pumped Storage Project in 1968 the Board removed the old turbines and generators in the B. A. C.'s powerhouse and replaced them with a 5 MW (5,000,000 watt) turbo-generator. This was designed to employ the water which otherwise would have run to waste during the building of the major scheme. This plant, called Foyers Falls, makes use of the original tunnel and pipelines of its predecessor.

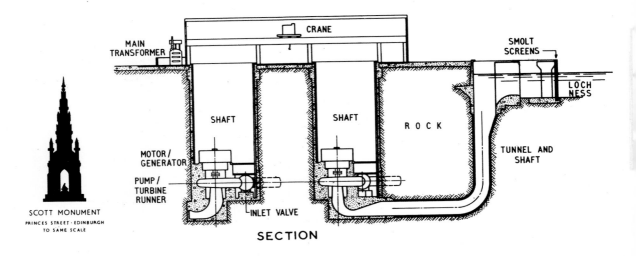

SCOTT MONUMENT
PRINCES STREET · EDINBURGH
TO SAME SCALE

SECTION

The underground pump-generators at the new Foyers power station

The next stage of the work consisted in preparing the ground for the new power-station. Unlike the B. A. C. who had a flat delta on which to raise their factory, the Hydro-Electric Board had to excavate a site from the steep banks of Loch Ness to the north-east. Early in 1970 a great rock fall took place here, sending eighty thousand tons of debris down onto the new platform. This compelled the building of a retaining wall and other extensive remedial work, none of which could have been anticipated. For technical reasons, which I shall explain later, the two great pump-generators had to be sited more than one hundred feet below the surface of Loch Ness. During the excavation of these massive shafts (the Scott Monument in Princes Street, Edinburgh could be comfortably hidden in either of them) the

Board's engineers were faced with considerable inflows of water, the same problem as had bedevilled Telford at the lower of the Fort Augustus locks. This delayed progress for many weeks. Major collapses of tunnel roofs also took place due, one presumes, to the chemical deterioration of the heavily faulted granite. Despite these difficulties, and many others which included national disputes, the Station was completed before its scheduled date on April 3rd 1975.

To appreciate it fully a word about its special function is necessary. Since I myself was quite ignorant about this until recently, I must speak carefully. At first glance the idea behind a Pumped Storage system appears inexplicable. It generates electricity by using the force of water from a high reservoir, discharges the water into a lower one and then pumps it up again. It only makes sense when you remember that the demand for electricity is not constant over the whole twenty-four hours and can fluctuate at any time. Electric current, once generated, cannot be stored. At night the demand is obviously lowest and then there is current to spare in the

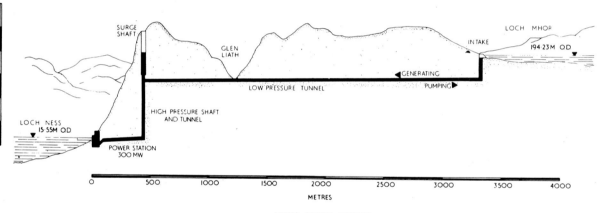

FOYERS PUMPED STORAGE

grid, that network of lines that serve the country's needs. The Foyers plant, like its counterpart at Loch Awe, is designed to take full advantage of this fact.

During the day, or if, for some reason, there is unusual demand, the two giant turbines, powered by the water from Loch Mhor, can send 300 megawatts (300,000,000 watts) into the national system. At night the water is pumped back using surplus electricity; then the specially designed turbines act as pumps and the generators become motors that drive them. The average motorist will be familiar with this reversal effect if his fan belt has broken. With the ignition on the generator continues to turn, drawing power from the battery, though in the opposite direction.

How Loch Mhor is connected to Loch Ness

Before I recently accepted the Board's invitation to see over the Foyers power station I found it hard to grasp the figures relating to its performance. From one of their pamphlets I learned that when generating the twin machines discharge water into the Loch at the rate of two hundred tonnes per second, and the effect of this, over a maximum eighteen hour period, would be to raise the surface level by up to eight inches. To absorb the rise a by-pass channel with control gates has been fitted to the south-eastern end of Telford's weir at Loch Dochfour.

A glance at the figure for the reverse process – that of pumping water back into Loch Mhor – prompted me to do a simple little sum. Given four rather broad assumptions I reached a staggering conclusion. *If* the rivers and burns that feed Loch Ness were diverted, *if* no rain should fall upon the Loch for the period of the exercise, *if* the pump intake could be set at its deepest point, and *if* a suitable river could be found to carry its waters to the sea, then Loch Ness could be drained of every drop of water by this pair of machines in one year and one hundred and fifty two days! What a chance for the sponsors of Operation Deepdrain (probably American) to solve one way or the other the mystery of the Loch Ness Monster.

Everything about this power station is on a colossal scale. On the top of a granite hill is the round, gaping mouth of a huge open pipe whose function is to absorb the sudden rise of pressure in the system when the plant switches from generating to pumping. At rest the water level in the pipe is that of Loch Mhor. The size of the tunnel that carries the water from Loch Mhor to Foyers (and back) can be judged by the pipe that surfaces for a short distance as it crosses Gleann Liath, the narrow valley that runs parallel to Loch Ness.

At the bottom of either of the shafts in the power station, well below the surface of Loch Ness, there are wonderful things, such as the hydraulically operated inlet valve which weighs eighty-five tons and is tested to resist pressure of six hundred pounds per square inch. The pumps and generators are enclosed but the gleaming steel shaft, which connects them, as fat as a great oak, is prominent; the whole assembly, with pump and electrical parts, weighs over 300 tons, and rotates at 273 revolutions per minute.

At either end of the building are the circular forebays through which the water comes and goes to the pump/turbines. Each furnished with four gates, they are entirely screened against the ingress of any but the smallest objects. It was pointed out to me that one of the advantages of this type of plant is the fact that any debris that is sucked against this screen during pumping is readily dispelled when the plant is generating. At the east end of the building are two enormous transformers. One of these, weighing 240 tons, has the distinction of being the heaviest load ever to pass through the Canal. Built in the north of England the machine was taken by sea to Nigg Bay, on the Cromarty Firth, and then transferred to a pontoon from which it was eventually unloaded at Foyers. Today it sits there, humming away to itself

The steel shaft, 'as fat as a great oak', at Foyers power station

The pipe from Loch Mhor to Foyers

loudly, its terminals connected to current-carrying metal rods as thick as a man's leg.

Pylons and their high tension cables are an undoubted blot on the landscape and it seems that nothing can be done to make them look less vile. Loch Ness has largely escaped this effrontery. From Foyers the towers stride away from the Loch at Bole-skine and the cables hang above the Inverfarigaig pass before marching through the remote woodlands and moorland to the north-east. They are horribly conspicuous at Loch Ceo Glais where they sing their new song above the stony heads of my two old watching ladies (see p. 130), but thereafter their impact is lost in the featureless country behind Loch Ashie.

When the Hydro-Electric Board inherited Loch Mhor from the B. A. C. they set out to increase the catchment area of Loch Mhor for now, in effect, they had two mouths to feed: the pumped storage plant and the 5 MW Foyers Falls conventional hydro-electric station. To bring in more water to the reservoir they tapped the River Fechlin (whose source is the remote Loch Killin) and piped its water across to the obscurely named River E which has always fed Loch Mhor. This was a pretty piece of engineering, and soundly conceived, but once again the great cataract at Foyers was the loser, as the Fechlin is, or was, the river's main contributory. During the renovation of the old earth dams at Loch Mhor's south-east end the loch was partly drained. As the water went down a crannog came to light. Its particulars were taken before it sank, once again, beneath the ripples. One cannot help being reminded of J. M. Barrie and Mary Rose's island.

From 1895 to 1975 Foyers was a centre of continuous employment on Loch Ness-side, which brought much benefit to local families. It was like Fort Augustus at the peak of the canal building, only it was to last much longer. But with the closing-down of the aluminium factory and the completion of the Pumped Storage scheme, all that has changed. The great idol that was the work of many hands needs only a very few to attend it. The advanced automation of this plant is of the kind that has turned the Luddites' uneasy nightmare into irreversible fact.

Long before the British Aluminium Company brought bauxite to Foyers another raw material was being smelted in Glenurquhart. Old records reveal that an iron manufactory existed there in 1634, funded by the laird of the day. Traces of the bloomeries were still in evidence fifty years ago. The policy of bringing the unprocessed material to the source of energy was applied here, as later at Foyers; ore was brought from the south, smelted in the glen and then returned as iron. Eventually the project failed (presumably due largely to transport costs and difficulties – there was no Caledonian Canal in those days) and the laird, Sir John Grant, lost his money over it as well as tens of thousands of birch trees – prized for their charcoal making properties – that were stripped from the hills.

Castle Grant, the home of 'Good' Sir James

With the Industrial Revolution well under way mining for metals was becoming very popular and mines were sunk on the flimsiest of evidence. Sir John, despite having burnt his fingers badly in the iron smelting, was greatly excited at a report – its origin is not recorded – that there was copper under his land in Glenurquhart. At once he gathered a large workforce and began to drive a shaft into the conglomerates on the west side of Drumnadrochit. Again it did not go well for him; what he was looking for does not exist in sedimentary rocks. But there was no halting the laird; one senses that in speculative mining, as in all gambling, it is not easy to stop when the investment has been heavy. In the end he had to give up – perhaps with the consolation prize of a few bits of copper pyrites, or Fool's Gold, from Heaven knows where – but the cost without return had been so great that he was forced to sell extensive lands elsewhere.

The burning of limestones and chalks for local use was a much sounder proposition. In 1770 the 'Good' Sir James Grant, anxious as ever to keep his tenants happy and occupied, and at home, made an agreement with a mason, one James Bollas, in which he guaranteed to take the lime from the mason at a fixed price, and Bollas was to pay him rent for the farm and buildings in which the kilns were situated. These were somewhere on the hill above the vilage of Milton, west of the Beauly road, and it is easy to find the quarries from which the limestone was mined. Even more obvious are the short walls and frayed edges of ancient peat cuttings on the moor above the farm at Culnakirk which is mentioned in the deed between laird and mason.

The extensive deer forest at Balmacaan which occupies an area of shaggy moorland, reedy lochans and low stony hills north-west of Loch Ness between the glens of Urquhart and Moriston was once a great sporting estate. The Grants, enriched by their succession to the earldom of Seafield, had lavished a great deal of money on this amenity, and the arrival of the American Bradley Martin (see p. 116) injected even more. Under the lease, he took over a headkeeper, sixteen general gardeners, four stalkers, nine ghillies and a game warden. A kennel man with a boy assistant were permanently engaged to rear pheasants and ensure that there never was a shortage of rabbits. Three other workers grew crops designed exclusively to give cover for the game. Enormous shooting parties, like private armies, were wont to issue forth for long days of slaughter. But it was never the same after Bradley died and his widow returned to the States in 1913. Behind Mealfuarvonie now, at the close of the 1980s, a few stags still roar throatily in Autumn and on that mountain's steep face, as on the gentler hills to the west, the chattering grouse explode beneath a walker's feet, but the day of the great forays is, regretfully or thankfully according to one's taste for these occasions, no more. Nowadays the Forestry Commission owns most of the estate.

Agriculture has long been practised in Glenurquhart, and in upper Glenmoriston. Flax, oats, barley, rye, and even some wheat, were grown here in the 16th century. A failure of the crops, for whatever reason, quickly led to severe famine. In 1782 there was one such catastrophe and it was indeed fortunate for the glenspeople that it came during the benevolent reign of the 'Good Sir James'. The laird sent up from London, 'ten tons of choice picked potatoes for seed, one hundred bolls of white pease for meal, and fifty bolls of seed oats'. Despite this gesture conditions in that year were grim; starving men and women lived on the blood of living cattle, nettles, berries and herbs.

The distilling of whisky and the brewing of ale were carried on with gusto around Loch Ness for both profit and pleasure; in secret places, almost or even to the present day. Such worthies as Donald Fraser of Abriachan thrived on the trade and the smuggling that went with it. In the 17th century almost every clachan (or hamlet) had an established still, often worked by the leading families of the parish, but the heavy hand of the Revenue finally suppressed the making of these ardent spirits on which no tax was paid. Yet in Urquhart two licensed breweries existed in the 19th century, and there was a distillery at Dores.

In 1756 the Trustees for Manufactories and Fisheries bought over one hundred acres of land from the Grants of Invermoriston and built a linen and woollen factory there. The Trustees' aim was, in part, akin to that of the present day Highland Development Board, to promote employment and business; but also to keep tempers in check and to discourage emigration by a largely discontented population. It gave steady employment to over fifty people for some years and at Drumnadrochit an earlier Sir James Grant, Sir Ludovick's father, put up a similar, though smaller, factory for the making of linen.

In 1803 Thomas Telford reported to the Government that many of the roads he had surveyed had, prior to 1742, been no more than tracks for Black Cattle and horses. During the 18th and 19th centuries huge herds of beasts from Urquhart and Glenmoriston, which had been wintered on the hills above these places and fattened on their summer pastures, were driven through Fort Augustus on their way to the chief Lowland markets of Crieff and Falkirk. They followed the military roads over the passes of Corrieyarrick and Drumochter, wild and inhospitable even to this day. At the other end of the Loch, cattle from places such as Muir of Ord crossed the River Ness at Bona before joining the Old Edinburgh Road (now the A9) at a point in Strathnairn, and thence south over the Slochd and Drumochter summits. The journey over these passes was necessarily undertaken in the autumn and early winter and the drovers – who sometimes worked on their own, assisted only by a dog – were men of a sturdy, heroic stamp. They had to be; in such places as the Corrieyarrick suitable parks for the beasts were far apart, bothies on the way were few, and there were long empty miles in which a drover might well be benighted in rain, mist or blizzard without shelter and, with the constant need to keep his herd together, often without sleep. Telford was well aware of the immense importance of sheep and cattle to the Scottish economy, a trade which, in his time, reached its peak of profitability during the Napoleonic wars. One practical example of his concern was his insistence on a thick layer of gravel on the roads most used for droving, to protect the hooves of the cattle from damage on their long treks.

10 The Monument to the Dragon

'YOU GOTTA monument to that old dragon yet?' I was dawdling on the Loch side with a friend on a fine summer's morning when an American stopped and asked me this awkward question.

The search for proof that a substantial aquatic animal unknown to science exists in Loch Ness really began in 1933. Before that the only written reference was set down by St Adamnan in his Life of St Columba when he describes an encounter between a ferocious water creature and his man of God. It is a miraculous tale only, which I have recountered on p. 35, invented to show the power of the Christian church over its pagan rivals. An hiatus followed which lasted for over twelve hundred years. If local people knew of the strange beast between neolithic times and 1933, they kept it a closely guarded secret. No mention is made of it by any of the occupants of Urquhart Castle – a viewpoint par excellence – between the 12th and 17th century. Thereafter Wade and his engineers were as silent as Cromwell and his troopers on the matter and nothing about it seems to have reached Telford's ears. All these people were closely associated with the Loch for long periods and maintained boats upon it.

Dr. Johnson was one of the Loch's earliest tourists. This great enquirer, with his unquenchable appetite for local colour, would have seized upon it, if only as food for his disparaging wit, but neither the governor at Fort Augustus nor the highlanders who accompanied the travellers in 1773 had anything to say about this alien creature. Nor does it appear anywhere in the songs and tales of local bards, although surely it is the very stuff of folklore. True, the kelpie or water horse maintained a legendary presence here but few lochs, even the smallest, were without that sinister denizen.

But from 1933 things changed. An article in the *Inverness Courier*, a greatly respected local paper, on May 3rd of that year aroused some public interest. Entitling his piece 'Strange Spectacle on Loch Ness' the writer linked a recent 'sighting' with some earlier ones. In a time when world news was undramatic, national newspapers took up the story to keep their readers happy. The road on the north side of the Loch was now more fit for motor traffic and the game of 'spot the monster' was born. A year later the London gynaecologist, R. K. Wilson, gave the thing a shape, and it was exactly the outline which the credulous craved: there was a longish neck and a small head with the hint of a hump behind. On the 21st April, two days after it was reputedly taken, The *Daily Mail* carried his photograph of it. Wilson, tongue in cheek, merely stated that it was something unusual that he had photographed in the Loch. He had no need to say more; a wide section of the reading public knew what a plesiosaur looked liked, and a surprisingly large number uncritically accepted it as such. Few bothered to study the picture, which might have been of anything between a toy and an otter's tail, or to refer to the relevant information in a book on prehistory. My own father, an intelligent, much travelled and worldly man, was one of these and I, an impressionable boy and a lover of the dramatic, was readily conditioned to his belief. To give a personal example of the general acceptance in the early 30s that there was 'something' in the Loch, let me quote from my diary for 20th June 1935: 'On our way home (after tea at the Foyers Hotel) we were lucky to see the wash of the Loch Ness Monster from Foyers Pier. A lot of other people watched it too.'

In those days before the war on our regular visits to the Loch we several times saw powerful washes, lines of humps and once a thin, attenuated neck passing like a great swan's behind winter trees which stood between road and water. Late one evening, after a moonlight descent from the crags above Abriachan, we heard a mighty splash in the Loch and scrambled down to the shore in time to see a ring of glittering waves emanating from a central turbulence. Not one of us doubted the origin of these phenomena; it would have been almost heretical to do so. We had every faith in our plesiosaur and although everybody wanted a good photograph it would only have brought final proof of something which we already knew to be true.

I had a 9.5 mm Pathescope projector in those days and I remember, somewhat hazily, a library film which my parents bought me. It was called *The Secret Of The Loch* and starred Sir Seymour Hicks in the role of an eccentric professor who is hot on our monster's trail. He has to put up with scepticism from those who hold the purse strings but in the end his faith is vindicated. The final scene which contained a miniaturised diver and a magnified lizard was always greeted with warm applause. *King Kong*, which was released in that Year of the Monster (1933), used an animated model to depict a plesiosaur in a swamp on the great ape's island and this must have played its part in preparing the public for Dr Wilson's photograph of the following year.

It was also in the late 1930s that R. L. Casey wrote his preposterous book *The Monsters Of Achanalt*. I have never met anyone who knew Mr Casey – nor did my father know anyone at the time – but I have often wondered since whether it was a puckish nature or sheer insanity that prompted him to write such an account. A resident of Strath Bran, the author described in considerable detail the movements of dinosaurs on Sgurr a Mhuilinn and Sgurr a Ghlas Leathaid, mountains on the south side of the Strath. As evidence of the credulous mood of the times – what difference was there between a plesiosaur in a loch and a dinosaur on a mountain, except that the latter was more easily verified? – many people known to us wasted their weekends in a fruitless search for these anachronistic survivors. Then the war came and there was no longer need of monsters to stir the public imagination.

In the 50s interest in the creature was slow to rekindle. Mere reports of sightings, even by the most reputable people, had little impact outside the immediate area, where it was still a matter of preaching to the converted. A further photograph, published in the national press, was necessary if popular support for the story was to be retained. It came in 1951, a print of poor quality showing three black objects floating a few yards off shore. This picture was a deliberate deception, and a bad one at that. I have no particular objection to hoaxers, unless they endanger lives or waste taxpayers' money, and my chief reaction on getting first-hand knowledge of the affair was surprise at how easily even experts can be duped. This amateurish invention was given the seal of approval by a leading zoologist as the 'most important picture'. At this time I was still one of the faithful and was ready to allow that anything as famous as the Loch Ness Monster was bound to have its imitators.

Tim Dinsdale's ciné film, taken in April 1960, was an important milestone. It generated wide-spread public interest when it was shown on Richard Dimbleby's *Panorama* programme on the 13th June 1960. We missed this TV feature at the time but I heard about it with excitement. Here was the evidence for which I had confidently waited since, as a boy of eleven, I had first set eyes upon the Loch. But when I saw it at a private viewing later I could not repress a sense of keen disappointment. I was doing a lot of messing about in small boats then, living with them you might even say, and here was simply another one of them. This was no monster but a ten- or twelve-foot wooden dinghy with a small outboard motor. I had seen the same thing too recently and too often, from every angle and from every distance, to be mistaken. The fact that I had met Dinsdale and recognised him as an intelligent

The late Tim Dinsdale in his camouflaged motor cruiser, fully equipped to hunt the Monster

man of the greatest integrity only added to my sad confusion.

Others did not share my view. Within a year a group of people who held a conviction that there was now more than ever a case to answer formed themselves into a body called the Loch Ness Investigation Bureau. They began their watch in 1962 at night, using powerful searchlights at the Clansman Hotel (beween Drumnadrochit and Abriachan), in the theory that the monster might surface in darkness. Nothing

came of it. Later they set up a base at Achnahanet, just west of Urquhart Castle, where cameras with telescopic lenses could command a wide area of the Loch's surface, and thence they daily sent vans, with roof-mounted cameras, to other points of vantage. All in all the coverage was considerable and the light-hearted, holiday mood of the volunteers in no way conflicted with a serious approach to their task.

Demands on my time and growing doubts prevented me from offering my services but we had many friends among the searchers. I had long been convinced that such a comprehensive scrutiny would shed a strong light on the mystery but after several years we knew no more than we had known before. When the evidence of the L. N. I. B. was shaken through a riddle of small mesh it left very little of substance, and the evaluation of the experts only served to cast a cloud of doubt upon much which had formerly been considered sacrosanct.

By 1968 I was rapidly becoming an agnostic in the religion of the Loch Ness Monster. Many of our friends, former believers, shared my sense of disillusion. It began to seem that the harder one looked for it the less likely it was to appear and this thought was reflected in the fact that fewer residents living within sight of the Loch had claimed to see it than had casual passers-by.

Tenacious attempts by scientists, dilettantes and promoters to prove the monster's case, for their various ends, continued throughout the 70s and do so to the present day. Many millions of words have been written and spoken about the why and wherefore of the Loch Ness phenomenon. While public interest justifies the time and expense, discussion and investigation will go on. The 'Official' Loch Ness Monster Exhibition at Drumnadrochit offers an admirably impartial pre-sentation of all the known speculations with excellent general exhibits about less controversial features of the Loch. It attracts many thousands of visitors each year.

These days I am an aggressive atheist in the matter and find it astounding that such wide-spread credulity can exist. To me the only phenomenon is that credulity itself. But, of course, it is not singular to Loch Ness. The truth of it is that mankind loves a mystery, be it real or contrived, and will go to great lengths to enjoy and support it.

There is, in fact, absolutely no reason why there should be anything out of the usual in Loch Ness. Apart from its length and depth it is quite ordinary; a land-locked fresh water lake fed by several small rivers and drained by a single short, fast-flowing one. It may well have existed before the last ice age and certainly developed much of the topography as we see it today between ten thousand and a million years ago. Then, ten thousand years ago, the action of the north-easterly moving glacier had deepened the great fault and left deposits of silt more than three hundred feet deep at the eastern end. As the ice continued to shrink, the now closed fissure filled with melt-water from the higher ground. Raised beaches in, for example, Glen Urquhart confirm that the water level of the Loch was periodically much higher than it is today, possibly due to thicker deposits at the Inverness end of the fault that have since been eroded away. This simple hypothesis, however, omits the fact that as the ice relented in the northern hemisphere the level of the sea rose, to be followed more slowly by regional land masses, relieved of the massive weight. Were it not for this it could be confidently stated that since the last glacial episode Loch Ness has not been open to the sea.

Perhaps it has not. On this question expert opinion seems to be divided. It is true that no traces of salinity have been found or any fossil remnants of marine life in the deep sediments. Either way it doesn't greatly affect the 'no monster' theory. What is crucial to the argument is the obvious-even-to-the-layman fact that no living creature could have survived prolonged entombment in an ice-filled Great Glen fault or in the frozen sea around it. If you were to put a live lizard in your Deep Freeze you wouldn't seriously expect to take it out and bring it back to life a quarter of a million years, or more, later! I don't really think it requires special intelligence to say that anything that now inhabits Loch Ness must have entered it at the end of the Pleistocene (or Plasticine as some abominable schoolboy is said to have called it) or during the current Holocene Age that began some ten millennia ago.

During these periods, and even well before them, marine life was much as it is today. Only marginal development of such species has taken place since then. Even if the seas had flooded the Loch Ness basin they wouldn't have left anything unexpected behind. Apart from its alleged monstrous occupant everything in Loch Ness – fish, eels, otters, occasional seals – are appropriate to a large body of fresh water in the Scottish Highlands or elsewhere in the British Isles.

People who favour the 'once open to the sea' theory have, from time to time, come up with some pretty odd suggestions. One is that the monster is a giant squid. Now this fellow's normal habitat is the North Atlantic where he sometimes reaches a length of thirty-five feet. His drawback as a candidate is that he doesn't in the least resemble anything that anyone has seen; apart from that he is a member of the Mollusc family, or a class of this, the Cephalopoda, which, by virtue of its physiology, doesn't take at all kindly to a change from salt to fresh water. On the other hand the squid is a powerful swimmer and is capable of changing its colour to match its background. This ability, at least, supports the claim for its candidature in that the monster of Loch Ness is very seldom seen!

Of the Amphibia, the newt has a pleasingly evocative shape but is rather on the small side. Even the most myopic observer could hardly take it for a thirty-foot-long water beast. The Giant Salamander reaches about five feet in length and slightly resembles its ancestors, who had long bodies and tails and four limbs each with five digits. The Salamander lives in the Far East, and those long-bodied ancestors became extinct two hundred millions years ago, so I don't think we should seriously

*The Plesiosaur, whom some see as
the forebear of the Monster*

back him as a claimant for the title.

Is it then a mammal? If this is the case, there would be no mystery. Dolphins, for instance, are pure exhibitionists who would attend the passage of every boat through the Loch with their show of almost embarrassing good humour and friendliness. Not a single day would pass without multiple sightings; they would be as little remarked as sheep beside Highland roads. So this fact alone positively excludes them, which is a pity for the dolphin could function in the Loch, a fact known to monstrologists who propose to use them to hunt their unknown cousin with sonar-triggered cameras and strobe-flash strapped to their sides. But it certainly won't be a case of set a dolphin to catch a dolphin.

Turning to the reptiles, we get very near to the sensitive core of the dispute, or its lunatic fringe if we are blunt. Nowadays the crocodile is the largest surviving member of the order, but in days long gone by reptiles grew to immense sizes. The preposterous idea that our monster might be a modified plesiosaur was born with Dr Wilson's photograph which by chance or design fitted artists' impressions of how that creature might have looked. The idea was nurtured and kept in front of the public gaze by further, though inferior, fake photographs, comic picture post-cards, and in a more general way by books and films such as *The Lost World*. In 1969 the Mirisch company created a life-size model of a plesiosaur-type creature for its production of *The Private Life of Sherlock Holmes*. A smaller edition of this may be found in the Hotel pond at the Official Exhibition, a light-hearted touch which belies the serious study within the Exhibition's walls.

Most remarkable of all has been the flirtation by well-known zoologists with this incredible theory. To me, though admittedly a complete layman, it seems unable to survive two indisputable objections. Firstly the study of fossil remains clearly shows that the plesiosaur became extinct in the Eocene period, 70 million years ago. When this point is made to them people are inclined to say, 'What about the coelacanth.' The comparison is, of course, irrelevant. The coelacanth is a fish, not a reptile. Because it was only known for a long time by its fossil remains it was thought to be extinct. In fact it has been living in the deep waters off the Coast of East Africa ever since it evolved in Devonian times 400 million years ago. Living in an unchanging environment, it was able to survive with a minimum of evolutionary adjustment.

The plesiosaur was a reptile, not a fish. Like all reptiles it was cold blooded and if, to make a hypothetical point, a live member of the order were introduced into Loch Ness's water at a temperature of 5–6 degrees Celsius, it would rapidly die or else go into a state of hibernation. Yet we are sometimes asked to believe that such a creature, intolerant to a chill that even man can only just stand, survived a succession of ice ages that covered the northern hemisphere. The idea is almost too absurd to merit mention at this length, and I only do so to underline the state of hysterical excitement into which a few photographs of a 'head and neck' and associated auto-suggested 'sightings' have thrown even the most sophisticated and cautious examiners.

Why do so many people, including those of the highest integrity, take the thing seriously? I believe that their case rests on two general supports: misinterpretation and auto-suggestion. Now I am referring to 'sightings' that were not accompanied by photographs. With all photographs I am also unimpressed, seeing them variously as pictures of natural objects, or contrived attempts at deception. The wake of a boat that has been allowed to vanish behind a point or building falls into the last category. I think it is also fair comment to say that underwater photographs and sonar scans have so far failed to narrow the gap between fiction and fact.

I must tell here, not to my very great credit, of a little light-hearted experiment which a friend and I conducted a few years ago in a lay-by on the A 82 on the Inverness side of Drumnadrochit. On a busy August afternoon we set up a camera on a low wall. The Loch was fairly rough, stirred by a fresh north east wind, and the wakes of a trio of trawlers were churning up some pleasantly suggestive material. The mere presence of the camera produced small public response – people recording the scenery are a common enough sight – until we began to engage in pantomime, pointing excitedly out into the Loch and panning the camera with gusto. Almost at once several cars turned off the road into the layby and disgorged their occupants.

The mood of the onlookers was essentially credulous. In answer to a battery of questions we stated that we had been attracted by the sight of a single large hump half way across the Loch. By now the last of the trawlers was a dark speck beyond Urquhart Castle, but the criss-crossing and rebounding wakes suggested not one but a school of monsters. Less than half of the audience had cameras but these were soon put to good account and it was easy to imagine the pleasure and argument that any clear photographs would later bring.

When all the films were used up – by then the crucial wake effects had merged into a general, less interesting, turbulence – we, as the first persons on the scene, were questioned more fully. We stuck to our original story, stating it briefly, for we were now most anxious to find in what way our companions had interpreted the scene. What we picked up in the general conversation that followed was interesting indeed. About a quarter of the assembly denied seeing anything other than a stormy loch, but their attitudes were less sceptical than resentful; one or two blamed short-sightedness and hoped that something would show up in their photographs. Of the others all were unanimous in claiming that they had seen long, dark bodies, undulating humps. Two men, sharing a pair of good binoculars, contended strongly that they had made out a thrashing tail and side flippers. As an example of mass misinterpretation the whole incident was remarkable, but for me the response of two quite different individuals was of special significance. A middle-aged lady with a Yorkshire accent told my friend that if her sister hadn't seen it too she wouldn't have believed her eyes. From that I later concluded that had the lady been on her own, even after witnessing our base antics, she mightn't have recognised the beast in the wave. Then, just as the party was breaking up, I noticed a lad of about ten who was leaning on the wall while he scribbled diligently on a small sketch pad. Unable to restrain myself I walked over and took a look at what he was doing. It was excellent: I was sure he would have a future as an artist. He had set down a graphic impression of Dores Point and the village, with Essich moor behind. With a quick, sure hand he had sketched in such details as tree clumps, fields and houses. In the time he had taken it was uncanny.

More uncanny too was the object he had drawn where the Loch had been roughest. It was a perfect plesiosaur. The oval hump, the stout neck breasting the waves, the flat head in profile: all were there. When he saw me looking at it he glanced up and said: 'That's right, isn't it?' I had to reply, 'Yes – if that's what you saw'. 'That's what I saw all right', he replied steadily. 'Didn't everybody?'

It is not difficult, then, to encourage people unversed in identification to see something which they want to see; the human mind under strong emotion, stress or excitement may produce its own pictures which can overprint the eye. The evidence of eye-witnesses to sudden and violent events, if these are unfamiliar to them, is notoriously unreliable. Tragic air disasters are cases in point; onlookers are often convinced that they have seen flames coming from air liners, or wings falling off them, when such embroideries, sincerely reported, are later shown to be imaginary.

In my second personal anecdote I am going to tell of a case where an image was so powerfully suggestive that it overcame, albeit briefly, a rigid disbelief. In the summer of 1970 Eustace Maxwell, brother of Gavin Maxwell who had sadly died in the previous year, had put a powerboat on Loch Ness in furtherance of a long-standing ambition – to track down and identify the Monster. Eustace, who was often our guest, was a firm believer and I was at the height of my disbelief; we spent a lot of time warmly disputing the matter. I did not, however, allow my scepticism to prevent me from enjoying his company or the brisk performance of his fine craft. Eustace had fitted a modest sonar device to the boat, which was called *Black Pearl* and the interesting, if expected, data this produced added an extra dimension to our stimulating voyages.

On that particular morning Loch Ness was dead calm. There was an uncanny clarity about the atmosphere and the Loch seemed squeezed and narrowed by the apparent closeness of the hills. The water was black and a colourless sky hinted strongly that rain was on the way. Accompanied by my eleven-year-old daughter Jane, we launched a rubber dinghy and reached *Black Pearl* which was anchored a hundred yards out in Urquhart Bay. On such an ideal surface the powerboat lifted easily on to the plane and hissed across the water like a diamond cutting glass. We were enjoying its fine, free powerful motion to the full when the engine suddenly spluttered and stopped. The boat fell from the planing position with a whoosh. Eustace, remembering that we had not checked the fuel that morning said 'Damn!' and pressed the starter more in hope than expectation. The engine caught and we resumed our racing angle but our skipper was a prudent man. 'Better turn back,' he said, 'while she's still going. We need fuel anyway.' Executing a tight turn we began to race back the way we had come.

We were somewhere in the middle of the Loch when the engine stopped again.

We flopped heavily onto the water. Repeated pressing of the starter only produced a surly whine. 'I'll have a look' I said, 'maybe it's something simple.' I knelt down beside the offending machine and began to fiddle. I was on the point of tightening a terminal on the low tension circuit when I heard Eustace Maxwell say 'Good God, look at this!' in a reverential voice. He and my daughter were staring wide eyed at something which was happening behind *Black Pearl*'s stern. What I saw there caused me to have a very singular mental experience. Like an old person who remembers his youth but not yesterday's lunch, I had forgotten my recent mood of passionate denial and was back in the days of confident expectation when I had known that, sooner or later, I would see the monster of Loch Ness. But never, in the wildest of my dreams, as close as this!

The creature was rising out of the Loch some twenty yards behind me. So swift had been its surfacing that its great dark hump was still concealed beneath a welter of black, cascading water. It was moving slightly away from us with a steady, powerful motion. The shock of this manifestation was so intense that the two thoughts most appropriate to the moment – my daughter's safety and the camera next to me on a seat – had no place in my mind. There was room there only for unbearable excitement at the prospect of further and final revelation.

It never came; but nor did our illusory creature execute a crash dive. It had been real, so real that a man might swear his life upon it, for less than the space of a minute, but as its evocative shape grew amorphous we saw it for what it truly was. The collision of water displaced by *Black Pearl*'s second return from the planing position with our outward wake had created a 'standing wave'. I had heard about such interference effects as the true origin of a host of sightings but had never realised their unique power to deceive. It was a subdued trio who returned to refuel *Black Pearl* at Temple Pier; even my irrepressible daughter was silent. It was as though we had been in the company of a celebrated magician who had just shown us the whys and wherefores of his skills.

Having given my unequivocal opinion of what it isn't – that is, a large aquatic creature unknown to zoologists except by its fossils, or even totaly unknown – and having affronted the faithful by my dogmatism, it behoves me to suggest what it is that they actually see. My own experience and observations have convinced me that by far the greatest number of 'sightings' arise from the misinterpretation of simple wake effects or, in striking cases (such as the event I have just related), the complex combination of wave forces: nothing more. As many people who visit Loch Ness are fresh to the workings of a great inland lake, they are the more easily taken in. My first anecdote shows that when the seeds of an impression are fertilised by propaganda they proliferate very readily. Familiar living things such as otters, flights of ducks or birds and even the occasional seal (a common seal has recently been tracked as far west as Fort Augustus) are a basis of a minority of the reports.

Loch Ness

Stags and horses have been known to swim in the Loch. A burst of gas from decaying vegetation is an infrequent phenomenon and floating trees are not hard to identify as inanimate objects. In a misty atmosphere any of these things appear much larger than they are (a hare on a hill can look as big as a deer in mist) and the viewer's sense of distance gets easily confused. Apart from the huge number of honest people who see what they see and are genuinely perplexed by it there is a small core which consists of jokers, liars and the mildly disturbed. Some claim to see the beast with the same regularity as did Mr Casey when he watched his languid dinosaurs on the Strath Bran hills. If I were the counsel for the prosecution I would say to these, 'No further questions,' and leave it to the jury.

On that fine summer's morning my American questioner was still waiting for his answer. I sensed that he was having a little fun at my expense, and I mildly resented it. No matter what my own views were on the matter he had no right to imply that our 'dragon' was dead! So I put on a foolish face and muttered some rustic words, and after a little time he seemed satisfied, got into his car and drove away.

Index